CRIMES AND MISDEMEANOURS

Tales from Sheffield and Beyond

DAVID BENTLEY

ALD
Sharrowvale Road
Sheffield

By the same Author

Select Cases from the Twelve Judges' Notebooks

English Criminal Justice in the Nineteenth Century

Victorian Men of Law

The Sheffield Hanged, 1750-1864

Sheffield Murders, 1865-1965

First Published in Great Britain by ALD, Sharrow Vale Road, Sheffield in 2005

Copyright David Bentley September 2005

The right of David Bentley to be identified as the Author of this work has been asserted by him in accordance with the Copyright Designs and Patents Act, 1998

All rights reserved. No part of this publication may be reproduced, stored in a retrieval system, or transmitted in any form or by any means electronic, mechanical, photocopying, recording or otherwise without the prior permission of the copyright owner.

David Bentley is a circuit judge. Born in Sheffield and educated at King Edward VII School, Sheffield, University College, London and the University of Sheffield, he practiced at the bar in Sheffield from 1969 until his appointment to the bench in 1988. He took silk in 1984. He has a doctorate in nineteenth-century legal history and is the author of books and articles on the subject. He lives in Sheffield with his wife and two sons.

Foreword

This book is a collection of legal tales, some relating to Sheffield and its surrounding district, others relating to the way the law, and the criminal law in particular, was administered in the eighteenth and nineteenth centuries. A good number caught my eye while I was carrying out other historical research. I hope others will find them as interesting as I did when I first read them.

I would like to thank my friend, Patrick Robertshaw, for reading the proofs and for his valuable suggestions as to their improvement. I have been greatly helped by the staff of the Sheffield Local Studies Library and the Inner Temple Library. The team at ALD have done their usual first class job and I am grateful to them all.

David Bentley

CONTENTS

Foreword v

Part 1 Tales from Sheffield and Beyond

1. The Nottingham Captain: Jeremiah Brandreth and the Pentridge Rising 3

2. Sheffield's Chartist Martyr, Samuel Holberry 12

3. The Wardsend Cemetery Riot, 1862 22

4. Sheffield Prisons 32

5. Derbyshire's Lord Chief Justice 37

6. The Padley Martyrs 43

7. Emily Swann 45

8. Ethel Major 55

Part 2 Judges behaving badly

8. Sir Jonah Barrington 65

9. The Shropshire Coroner 73

10. Dickens and the Bench 83

11. William Ramshay 87

12. Death in Nottingham 96

Part 3   Petticoat perjury

13. Will you hang him or marry him?....................................103

14. The Vicar's daughter..107

15. The Trials of the Rev Henry Hatch................................113

Part 4   Gallows Tales

16. Going to see a man hanged 133

17. Martha Browne's body: A Wessex tale 137

18. The Medical Hangman 142

19. The last public execution in Yorkshire 148

20. York private executions 152

21. Executions in literature 155

Index..167

PART 1

TALES FROM SHEFFIELD AND BEYOND

The Nottingham Captain[1]

In England, the end of the Napoleonic wars was followed by a severe economic depression.

'There probably never was a period of our history in which there was so much wretchedness and consequent disaffection among the English lower classes as in the four or five years that immediately followed the close of the [war]'.[2]

Popular disaffection found expression in spasmodic outbreaks of machine breaking, rick-burning and rioting. In December 1816, following a huge rally in Spa Fields, rioters attempted to seize the Tower of London. The ruling classes who had, ever since 1789, feared a French style revolution, were becoming daily more jittery and when, in January 1817, the Prince Regent was mobbed and the windows of his coach smashed, as he returned from the opening of Parliament, government panic knew no bounds; legislation was rushed through suspending *habeas corpus* and proscribing reform associations and clubs as unlawful combinations. How unwilling the authorities had become to countenance even peaceful protest

---

[1] E P Thompson, *The Making of the English Working Class*, Penguin Books Ltd, London, 1977, pp 720-25, 727-34; J L & B Hammond, *The Skilled Labourer*, Allen Sutton Publishing Ltd, 1995, pp 360-62, 368-70, 374; W B Gurney, *The Trial of Jeremiah Brandreth & Others*, Butterworths, London, 1817.

[2] Sir Joseph Arnould, *A Memoir of Thomas, First Baron Denman*, Longman Green, London 1873, vol. i, p. 105; see also Lord Byron, during a Lords' debate on a Nottingham Frame Breaking Bill which sought to repress increasing discontent by increasing severity, 'never have I seen such squalid wretchedness as I have seen since my return to the heart of a Christian country.' (cited by Arnould, i, 104). By 1817 the condition of the poor was desperate: 'The summer of 1816 had been one of the worst ever known in England, the rain had been incessant and the harvest was a complete failure. In the next winter and summer the price of bread was as high as it had even been during the worst years of the war; the profits of trade had been greatly reduced, the demand for our manufactures had diminished and numbers of operatives were thrown out of employment' (Arnould, i, 106).

was shown in March, when a group of textile workers[3] set out to walk to London with a petition for the Prince Regent; they were arrested before they had even reached Stockport.

As part of its strategy to crush opposition and prevent revolution the Government employed spies to infiltrate dissident groups and organisations. Of these one, known to posterity as 'the spy Oliver,' made it his business, not merely to gather information, but actually to incite insurrection.[4] In May and early June, 1817 he was active in Nottingham and the West Riding, both areas with a strong Luddite tradition. Having won the confidence of local radicals, he sought to recruit their support for a rising which was planned in the metropolis. One his dupes was unemployed Nottingham stocking- maker, Jeremiah Brandreth.[5] Believing Oliver's assurances that June 9 would see large-scale risings in London and the north, he hurried to Pentridge, a small village 24 miles south of Sheffield to recruit a force to march on Nottingham.[6]

On the 8th using the *White Horse* public house as his base he began recruiting. That Sunday he held court there all day, talking

---

[3] Known to history as 'the blanketeers'.
[4] Oliver was a building surveyor who had been sent to the Fleet Prison for debt, and it was from there that he was recruited as a Home Office spy. Edward Baines, the editor of the *Leeds Mercury*, described him as 'a prototype of Lucifer whose distinguishing characteristic is first to tempt and then to betray;' Cobbett *(Political Register*, May 16, 1818) said of him that he left 'his victims in the traps he set for them.'
[5] Brandreth is variously described as having been born in Ireland, Exeter and - the most probable – at Wilford near Nottingham, but nothing is known of his parentage or early life. For some time he was in the army, but shortly before the attempted rising he lived with his wife and children in Sutton-in-Ashfield where he worked as a framework knitter (*Dictionary of National Biography*). In 1803 he was present when Colonel Despard was hung, drawn and quartered for high treason and it is thought that, in 1811, he took part in Luddite activities.
[6] On June 6, Oliver had been seen by a reformer in a Wakefield hotel in the company of a servant of the local army commander, General Byng, giving rise to rumours of treachery. The news that there were suspicions against Oliver reached Nottingham, but not Brandreth, on the 7th.

openly of revolution and of the need to overthrow the government.

The following night there would, he told his listeners, be risings in London and the north. In London, the rebels who numbered 50,000 would seize the Tower and overthrow the government. He himself would lead a rising of men from Pentridge and surrounding villages. They would set out for Nottingham at nightfall and at 2 am would rendezvous at Nottingham forest, on the north side of the town, with contingents from Sheffield, Manchester and the north. The combined force would then descend on and take Nottingham. Once in the town, there would be plenty of rum and 100 guineas for each man. There would even be a pleasure trip on the Trent. 'The clouds from the north' would, he assured his audience, swamp all before them. During the day there was a stream of visitors to the *White Horse* and by evening 200 men or thereabouts had been recruited.[7]

At around 8 pm on the Monday night, Brandreth and his lieutenant Ludlam proceeded to a series of meeting points where they were joined by contingents from Pentridge, South Wingfield, Swanwick, Ripley and Butterley. There were stocking framers, quarrymen and workmen from Butterley Iron Works (the recent dismissal of ten workers there had helped to boost recruiting). They were armed with scythes, spikes (sticks with nails through them) and cudgels but had few guns. As they marched, they stopped at local houses and farms, demanding that the occupants

---

[7] Two constables, named Martin and Asbury, were present in the *White Horse* during the recruiting but, out of fear, did not report what they had seen or heard, Brandreth having threatened to kill anyone who told.

surrender their firearms, which most reluctantly did. In some cases, they forced a man from the house to join their ranks. At South Wingfield, one householder, the widow Hepworth, barred her doors to them. Enraged Brandreth went round to the back of the property and fired a shot through the kitchen window, killing a servant who was hiding behind a door. Fearing for her life, Mrs Hepworth handed over a gun, which she had been hiding in her cellar.

Some of the group made a diversion to Butterley ironworks, seeking recruits, but the gates were barred and they were turned away. They rejoined the main party at Greenwich[8] and the whole force now began to move south two abreast, with Brandreth at its head. As they approached Ripley they were joined by a contingent from Swanwick. At Ripley their numbers were further swelled. At Codnor they knocked up the landlord of the *Glass House* public house and demanded ale. The bill which came to £1 8s was left unpaid, Brandreth assuring the landlord that he would get his money within a fortnight. From Codnor they marched to Langley Mill on the county border, still seeking to add to their store of weapons and press recruits as they went.

By now they were well behind schedule. They had been due to meet the northern contingents at the forest at 2 am, but much time had been lost collecting weapons and, as dawn began to break, they were still about seven miles from the rendezvous. Some were starting to lose heart. It had been raining heavily all night and, although a messenger sent ahead to Nottingham to spy

---

[8] A hamlet immediately to the east of Ripley.

out the land had returned with encouraging news that the town was theirs for the taking,⁹ it was worrying that there was still no sign of any of the promised forces from the north.¹⁰ Men began to slip away which provoked from Brandreth a threat to shoot any who deserted.

Meanwhile, in Nottingham, the authorities, who were well aware what was afoot, had not been idle and, at Giltbrook south of Eastwood, the insurgents were met by a force of dragoons. What happened then was later described by a magistrate who was riding with the soldiers

> ' ... about a mile before we reached Eastwood we came in sight of the mob who, though at near three quarters of a mile distance from us, no sooner saw the Troops than they fled in all directions, dispersing over the fields and throwing away their arms; they were pursued for a considerable time and finally driven out of this county and into Derbyshire ... they did not fire a single shot and seemed only intent on escape.'

Some were captured at once. Others were flushed out of woods and hedgerows. In all about 48 were taken. Brandreth was among those who escaped. He made his way to Bristol where he attempted in vain to book a passage to America. Six weeks after the rising he was captured at a house in Nottingham.¹¹

Of those arrested, 35 were committed by the magistrates to the county gaol at Derby to await trial on a charge of high

---

⁹ This was a gross exaggeration. There had been disturbances in Nottingham that night and, at around 11.30 pm, a man, named Roper, who was making his way to his house on the edge of the forest, saw a group of about 100 men, armed with pikes, drawn up in a line two deep. But that seems to have been the extent of the disaffection.

¹⁰ On the night of June 8/9 several hundred clothing workers, mainly from Holmfirth, marched on Huddersfield, but melted away after encountering a small party of soldiers with whom they exchanged shots; some were apprehended and brought to trial in July but the jury, no doubt influenced by disclosures in the *Leeds Mercury* of Oliver's activities in the area, refused to convict.

¹¹ He remained in concealment until £50 was offered for his capture, upon which a friend betrayed him to the government (*Dictionary of National Biography*).

treason.[12] In October 1817, a special Commission consisting of four judges, Richards CB, Dallas J, Abbott J and Holroyd J, was sent down to Derby to try them. The proceedings got under way on October 17 in the Shire Hall in St. Mary's Gate, with Brandreth the first to be tried. Serjeant Cross and Thomas Denman, the future lord chief justice, appeared for Brandreth and for the two other principal accused, Turner[13] and Ludlam.[14] The treason alleged in the indictment was 'levying war against the King' and the line which Denman decided to take on behalf of Brandreth was that the facts proved by the Crown amounted not to treason by levying war, but merely to an aggravated riot, a submission which he supported by copious citation of legal texts and authorities. His speech earned considerable praise but it cut no ice with the chief baron. 'Armed insurrection for the purpose of effecting a change of government amounted 'in construction of law' to a levying of war against the king,' he told the jury. Armed with this direction, the jury retired and 25 minutes later returned with a verdict of guilty.

Turner and Ludlam then took their trials. On their behalf Denman tried a different tack, arguing that they had been under the spell of their captain and likening Brandreth to Byron's Corsair

There breathe but few whose aspect might defy
The full encounter of his searching eye

---

[12] They were kept for weeks on a diet of bread and water and refused all visits. Their relatives sold everything, down to their beds, to raise money for their defence.
[13] William Turner was a 46-year-old stonemason from South Wingfield.
[14] Isaac Ludlam, also of South Wingfield, was a 52-year-old stonegetter.

There was a laughing devil in his sneer
That raised emotions both of rage and fear

For all its eloquence the plea was not enough to save his clients.

Following the trial and conviction of a fourth accused, George Weightman, 19 further defendants, having received assurances that their lives would be spared, pleaded guilty, whilst charges against the remaining 12 were dropped.

On October 25, the 23 who had been convicted were brought up before the chief baron for sentence. 'Your object,' he told them

> '*was to wade in the blood of your Countrymen, to extinguish the Law and the Constitution of your country, and to sacrifice the property, the liberties and the lives of your fellow subjects, to confusion and anarchy and the most complete tyranny. God be praised, your purpose failed.*'

This said, he ordered all of them to be hung, drawn and quartered.[15] But of the 23, only Brandreth, Turner and Ludlam were left for execution, the death sentences on the remaining prisoners being commuted either to transportation or imprisonment.[16]

The execution took place thirteen days later outside the county gaol, watched by a large crowd. The law required that they be drawn to the place of execution on a hurdle and so, on

---

[15] The sentence in full was 'that you, and each of you, be taken from hence to the gaol from when you came, and from thence be drawn on a hurdle to the place of execution and be there hanged by the neck until you be dead and that afterwards your heads shall be severed from your bodies and your bodies divided into quarters and disposed of as His Majesty shall determine.'

[16] 11 were sentenced to transportation for life; three to transportation for 14 years; one to 2 years' imprisonment, two to 1 year and three to 6 months; ten of transports sailed on the *Tottenham* and the remaining four on the *Isabella*, reaching Sydney in September and October 1818 respectively; many of them ended up settling in Australia.

emerging from the prison chapel just after midday, the three condemned were taken to the prison yard and there placed in turn upon a wooden hurdle, which was dragged around the yard for several turns by a horse. This bizarre preliminary having been completed, they were taken through the prison and led out on to the scaffold which had been erected in Nun's Green.[17] None of them sought to address the crowd although, Ludlam was heard to shout 'This is all Oliver and the Government.' They were pinioned and ropes placed around their necks. The chaplain said a prayer in which they all joined, they were hooded and drop fell. After their bodies had been hanging for half an hour, they were cut down. Brandreth's head was then placed on a block at the front of the scaffold and, with some difficulty, severed from his body.[18] Picking it up by the hair, the masked hangman showed it to the crowd, crying 'Behold the head of Jeremiah Brandreth, the Traitor.' The bodies of Turner and Ludlam were then subjected to the same grisly procedure. The crowd, many of whom had reacted with horror to the beheading, were spared the sight of the bodies being quartered, the Prince Regent having graciously remitted this part of the penalty. The corpses and the severed heads were then placed in coffins and, after dusk, were buried in St Werburgh's churchyard, Derby.

A feature of the trial, which has attracted much comment, was the absence of any reference to Oliver. Denman was well aware of the latter's role in the matter, and there were many who

---

[17] Cavalry stood on guard near the scaffold during the execution.
[18] The block can still be seen in the Derby Gaol Museum in Friar Gate; it is claimed that 'it is damp, always damp.'

had expected the defence to try and prove that he had been the instigator of the whole affair. Had they done so, it might well have affected the outcome. That they did no do so appeared all the more extraordinary given that as a result of his exposure in the *Leeds Mercury* in June 1817, the whole country knew of Oliver and his works, and given also that several reformers had declared their willingness to travel to Derby to testify as to his activities, even at the risk of incriminating themselves. Denman would later justify his decision on the ground that the law prohibited him from cross-examining his own witnesses, and claimed that, had he called such testimony, it would merely have added weight to the prosecution case. But this does not convince. Without evidence of Oliver's complicity, the accused had no hope of acquittal, so overwhelming was the Crown's case. So why not try and get in front of the jury the one piece of evidence which would be likely to excite sympathy? The Crown were desperate that Oliver's name should not be mentioned.[19] Why oblige them? What had the defence to lose by exposing him?

Brandreth and his two companions were not the last persons to be hung drawn and quartered; that unenviable distinction belongs to the Cato Street conspirators who were put to death in 1820.

---

[19] See PRO, H.O 42, 171 (October 19) where Litchfield the Treasury solicitor sets out the prosecuting strategy 'avoiding all questions about O and not ever giving them an opportunity of introducing his name' and (October 22) 'we have resolved not to bring forward any prosecution in which his name can be brought in question.'

At the time the fate of Brandreth and his companions attracted a good deal of sympathy[20] and in Pentridge (known today as Pentrich), the rising is still remembered, a series of ten commemorative plaques marking out a 'Revolution Trail.'[21]

Sheffield's Chartist Martyr: Samuel Holberry

In 1840, Samuel Holberry, a young Sheffield Chartist, was arrested for treason and was more than a little fortunate not to be put on trial for the offence. If he had been, he would have stood in peril of suffering the same grisly fate as had befallen Brandreth and the Cato Street conspirators.[22] He would also have been the first Sheffielder to die for treason since Charles Beaumond in 1602.[23]

Holberry was the son of a Nottinghamshire farm labourer who, after serving in the army, took work in the brewing trade. During a spell working in London he became involved in radical politics. A year or so before his arrest he had moved to Sheffield where he joined the local Chartists. Chartism was a popular movement which came to the fore in the 1830s, with the object of securing the enactment by Parliament of a People's Charter,

---

[20] Percy Bysshe Shelley, who witnessed the execution, made reference to the rising in his polemic *An Address to the People on the Death of Princess Charlotte* (1817); the Earl Fitzwilliam, the Lord Lieutenant of Yorkshire, wrote to Lord Sidmouth, the Home Secretary, blaming the rising on Oliver: 'He is considered the main spring from which every movement has taken its rise.' (*English Historical Documents, 1783-1832* (ed. A. Aspinall and E.A. Smith), Eyre & Spottiswood, London, 1959, p. 332; Cobbett in his *Political Register* asked 'What did Brandreth do more than was done by the Whigs at the Revolution?'; see also Charles Lamb's poem *'The three graves.'*
[21] The *White Horse* is no longer there (it was demolished almost immediately after the rising). Its site and that of Widow Hepworth's farm are marked by plaques.
[22] I.e. being hung, drawn and quartered.
[23] Executed at York for coining (then a form of treason).

granting full electoral rights to the working class.[24] It was particularly strong in the north of England and

> *for four years between 1838 and 1842 it kept the great industrial centres in uproar. Its strength fluctuated according to the state of trade and unemployment and it was severely weakened by the inability of its leaders to agree over tactics.*[25]

In September, 1838, a Chartist meeting in Paradise Square, Sheffield attracted a crowd estimated at 20,000. This would prove but a foretaste of things to come.

On July 12, 1839, a National Petition, bearing 1,250,000 signatures, was presented to Parliament by Birmingham MP and Chartist sympathiser, Thomas Attwood. The Commons rejected it by a vote of 235 to 46.

A section of the movement had from the first advocated armed insurrection and, after the failure of the National Petition, the number prepared to countenance the use of violence to enforce their demands grew sharply. In November, a group led by local draper and former magistrate, John Frost, marched on Monmouth with the object of freeing one of their leaders who was held in prison. They took the town hall but, after a fierce fight, were evicted from it by the military at a cost of 14 dead and about 50 wounded. Frost and the other leaders were arrested and put on trial for treason.

The failure of the Monmouth rising may have disappointed but it certainly did not discourage the Sheffield Chartists.

---

[24] The Chartists had six principal demands (the so called 'Six Points') universal adult manhood suffrage, annual parliaments, vote by ballot, equal electoral districts, abolition of the property qualification for MPs and payment of MPs.
[25] P Gregg, *A Social & Economic History of Great Britain*, Harrop & Co., London, 1950, p. 205.

Throughout 1839 they had been growing ever more militant. One of the tactics they employed was to hold silent meetings - large open-air meetings at which no-one spoke. Fearful of rioting, the local magistrates warned local leaders that they were breaking the law. When the warning was ignored the military were called in. On September 12, a silent meeting at Paradise Square was dispersed by hussars and, when it attempted to regroup, a combined force of police and soldiers moved in, making 36 arrests. The hussars were again in action two days later, putting to flight a group returning from a meeting at Skye Edge. All this was worrying enough for the magistracy but things were soon to take an altogether more serious turn.

In late 1839 a group in the town, led by Holberry, were busy arming themselves with weapons. Copying a practice used by the Wesleyans, they divided themselves into classes, which met at the houses of their respective leaders.[26] Leaders' meetings were held at a house in Figtree Lane. By the New Year they had settled on their plan. A rising would take place on January 12 in which the Town Hall and the *Tontine*[27] would be seized. Gun shops would be broken into and their stock seized and distributed. To neutralise the threat from the cavalry, cats (spiked steel balls) would be strewn in the streets and, to draw the police and soldiers out of the town centre, the cavalry barracks and the houses of

---

[26] These houses were scattered across the town.
[27] The *Tontine* stood in Dixon Lane. Its history is given in Hunter's *Hallamshire*: 'On 29 September 1785 it was resolved at a meeting held in Sheffield to erect a commodious inn on a site 'where the Castle Barn now stands' at a cost of not less than £4,000, this sum to be raised by a Tontine. Each subscriber nominated a life during the continuance of which he was to receive an equal share of the rents and profits.' It was demolished in 1850 and the site used for the construction of the Norfolk Market.

magistrates and other gentry living on the outskirts would be fired. If the attack on the Town Hall was repulsed, the insurgents were to start firing the town.[28] Contingents from Rotherham, Ecclesfield, Eckington, Grenoside and Handsworth would join the rising. There would also be simultaneous risings in Nottingham and Dewsbury. Although the number of insurgents would be but modest, it was expected that, as soon as an initial success had been gained, all Sheffield would rush to join them and be 'liberated'.

Despite the fact that Holberry had threatened to kill anyone who backed out, the plot was betrayed. In early January John Bland, the chief constable of Rotherham, having heard rumours that trouble was afoot and anxious to nip it in the bud, put pressure on the Rotherham class leader, James Allen, to act as his spy. Allen who had little stomach for violence agreed. After attending meetings at the house in Figtree Lane, he reported back that a rising was being planned. Bland passed on what he had learned to Parker, the chief Sheffield magistrate, and Raynor, the surveyor of the town's police, but they dismissed the notion as fanciful. Bland, however, was convinced that Allen was on to something and he urged him to find out more.

On the evening of Saturday January 11, with the rising now but hours away, Bland's persistence paid off. Allen arrived hotfoot from a meeting in Figtree Lane with full details of 'time, place and plan.' There was clearly no time to lose and, having heard Allen out, Lord Howard, a Rotherham magistrate,

---

[28] 'Moscow the town' was Holberry's instruction.

immediately rode pell mell to Sheffield where he alerted Raynor. The latter acted with exemplary speed and vigour. A detachment of cavalry was despatched from the barracks to secure the streets while the police set about rounding up the ringleaders.

Holberry was arrested in bed at his house at 19, Eyre Lane; in the garret were large quantities of arms and ammunition. Thomas Booker was caught by a cavalry patrol in Crookesmoor standing near a pile of steel cats and armed with a dagger. When his home, at 4, Bennet Lane, was searched hand grenades and ball cartridges were recovered. Also arrested at the house were his son William and a youth named Foxall: both were sitting by the fire, fully dressed and looked as though they had just arrived. In a corner of the room was a gun which Foxall said was his. Troops and police officers also descended on the places where the insurgents had been instructed to muster, and put those who had gathered to flight (at Watery Lane a hundred or so men had assembled and there were fifty outside the Carver Street chapel).

At 5 a.m. a youth, named Samuel Thompson, was arrested in the street, armed with two swords and his dagger. Thompson's father, (also called Samuel), a well known Chartist, was arrested when officers searching his home found a dagger hidden in a basket of groceries.

During the course of the Sunday large quantities of abandoned weapons were found both in the town and on the outskirts. Several caches of weapons were also discovered.

The authorities' intervention had come just in the nick of time and, at the cost of a handful of police and civilian casualties, a conspiracy 'which…. had it been carried through would probably resulted in enormous mischief' was thwarted.

On Monday, January 13, Holberry, his wife, Thomas Booker, Booker's son William, Samuel Foxall and Samuel Thompson were brought before magistrates at the Town Hall for preliminary examination. The charge was high treason by levying war against the Queen. Solicitors, Palfreyman and Rodgers, appeared for the prosecution, the prisoners being unrepresented. A table in front of the bench was 'literally covered with pikes, daggers, firearms, combustilble and destructive materials.' The proceedings lasted three days.

Evidence was given by police officers of the arrest of Holberry and Thomas Booker and of the arms found in their possession upon arrest. Holberry had, they claimed, admitted that he was a Chartist who was for physical force and prepared to take life in defence of the Charter. Other witnesses gave evidence of the dispersal of armed insurgents who had mustered at Watery Lane and Carver Street, of attacks upon watchmen in Infirmary Road and Glossop Road, and of the weapons found abandoned the next morning. The most damning evidence against Holberry came, however, from Samuel Thompson junior and an 18-year-old Chartist, named William Wells. Both claimed to have been present at meetings in Figtree Lane, where Holberry had outlined the plan for the rising and given instructions as to the parts to be played by those present.

At the conclusion of the evidence the prosecution invited the court to discharge Mrs Holberry, conceding that there was no evidence against her (by this time the bench had at the prosecution's invitation also discharged Samuel Thompson senior – no doubt as a *quid pro quo* for the assistance the son had given to the Crown). They announced that they had decided to proceed on the charge of treason against Holberry and Thomas Booker alone. Both men were offered the opportunity to state their defence and to call witnesses. Holberry reserved his defence and Booker, after starting to proffer an explanation of his conduct, fell silent when he was told that he was doing himself more harm than good. The magistrates thereupon committed the pair to York to stand trial for high treason. They were conveyed from the Town Hall in a carriage and four, escorted by a squadron of dragoons.

On Friday, January 17, William Booker appeared in the dock along with six others men[29] charged with conspiracy and riot. Before the day was out the case against one of them had been dropped after witnesses testified that all he had done was to urge others to go home. By the following Monday the number of accused had risen to eight, two further men having been charged over the weekend.

The prosecution case was that all had agreed to take part in the rising and, to that end, had gone out armed in the early hours of Sunday morning. There was evidence from police officers of weapons being found on them or in their houses when they were arrested but, as at Holberry's committal, the most damning testimony came from two of their erstwhile companions, Thompson senior and Foxall. The hearing ended with the

---

[29] When on the Monday the treason charge against him was dropped, the magistrates had remanded him in custody.

magistrates committing all eight for trial, observing that two or three of them fortunate not to be facing a charge of high treason.

By the time Holberry and Booker appeared at York Assizes in March 1840, the threat of the death sentence, which had been hanging over them since committal, had been lifted, the prosecution having elected to proceed against them on the lesser and non-capital charge of conspiracy to riot. In January, Frost and six others, who had taken part in the Monmouth rising, had been convicted of treason and sentenced to be hung, drawn and quartered. There was widespread public protest not least at the barbarity of the mode of execution. On February 1, the Prime Minister, Lord Melbourne, announced that the sentences would be commuted to transportation for life. Frost's life having been spared, it would hardly go down well with a jury, still less with the public at large, for the Crown to seek the death penalty against the two Sheffield Chartists, given that the rising at Sheffield never really got off the ground whereas at Monmouth 14 people had lost their lives.

When those whom the magistrates had sent for trial were arraigned before Mr Justice Erskine, in the week of March 16, all but Holberry, Samuel Booker, his son William and two others, Murray and Duffy pleaded guilty to conspiracy to riot.

At the trial of the five who pleaded not guilty, the same evidence was led as had been given at the committal hearing. The case against them was in reality overwhelming and the jury brought back verdicts of guilty without leaving their box.

On the Saturday the defendants were brought up to receive sentence. Holberry was sentenced to 4 years' imprisonment, Samuel Booker and Duffy to 3 years, William Booker, Marshall and two others to 2 years and William Wells to one year.

The prison to which Holberry was sent to serve his sentence was the Northallerton House of Correction. Conditions there were harsh: prisoners were kept shackled and forbidden to speak to each other (the so called 'silent system'). During his first five months there, Holberry, although not sentenced to hard labour, was put to the treadmill. The regime soon took its toll; already troubled by swelling of the legs he began to display symptoms of consumption. In December 1840, a visiting prison inspector recommended that he be moved to a 'more airy location,' but nothing was done. Outside prison, his wife started a campaign for his release. Petitions were sent to the House of Commons. At first they were ignored but in August 1841, a letter from the Northallerton prison surgeon resulted in the House referring Holberry's case to the Home Secretary. The upshot of this was an order that he be transferred to York Castle. By now he was suffering from liver disease as well as consumption. Conditions at York were better than at Northallerton and at first it seemed that he might be on the mend. But he was not.

By Spring 1842, he was bedridden. Indeed, so concerned had the prison surgeon become at his condition that he wrote to the Home Office warning that he was likely to die if detained any longer. This letter persuaded the Home Secretary to grant the dying Holberry a pardon. But there was a final twist. It was a condition of the pardon that he should provide two sureties for his good behaviour for the five years following his release. This proved impossible to do and, on June 21 1842, while his young wife Mary was frantically trying to find the necessary sureties, Holberry died. He was 27- years- old.

His body was brought back to Sheffield to receive 'a martyr's funeral. [Huge] crowds lined the route' as the cortege wended its way 'from Attercliffe, where his body had lain in state at the cottage of Mary Holberry's parents, to the General Cemetery. There, amidst impassioned speeches by other Chartist leaders, [he] was laid to rest.'[30]

---

[30] J E Vickers, *A Popular History of Sheffield*, Applebaum, Sheffield, 1992 , p. 97. See also the description of the funeral in the *Sheffield Independent*, for July 2, 1842:

'The procession left Attercliffe about 2 30 headed by the band playing Pleyell's German hymn. Next came the hearse, funeral coaches and a few carriages succeeded by the Figtree Lane Chartists, who were headed by a large black banner with *'Thou shalt do no murder'* inscribed on one side and on the other *'Vengeance is mine, I will repay saith the Lord.'* [Then came] the O' Connor Chartists with the females going first. [They were followed by] ...the Chartists of the Political Institute headed by their Council; these were few in number but of much superior appearance, being well dressed, and wearing black scarves. They were accompanied by a white flag with the inscription *'Political Institute, Birks, Clayton and Holberry, martyrs of the People's Charter. The Lord hateth the hands that shed innocent blood.'*

The route was along the Wicker, High Street, Fargate, Coalpit Lane, South Street and Ecclesall Road. The mass that attended the procession continued to augment as it advanced. The walls along Ecclesall new road to the Cemetery were occupied by spectators some time before the procession reached it. The gates leading to the cemetery were kept closed by marshals and, when opened, there was a general rush to be admitted in which flowers plants and shrubs were trampled. After the service in the chapel and over the grave a hymn, composed for the occasion by John Henry Bromwich of Leicester, was sung to the tune of the Old Hundred (with copies on sale at a halfpenny). Messrs Harney and Parkes [O'Connor Chartists] proceeded to address the assemblage eulogising Holberry as a patriot, charging the Government with his blood and denouncing those who gave evidence against him at his trial. Thompson from the Vale of Leven followed. His speech was much more temperate. The procession then returned to town headed by the band as before. Pick-pocketing was practised during the proceedings. In the evening a meeting of several thousands was held in Paradise Square. They were addressed by the O'Connor orators and were called on to pass various resolutions including one strongly condemning [the Home Secretary] Sir James Graham in relation to Holberry's death. The meeting continued until about 9 30.'

Allen, who in the days after the rising had been kept under armed guard for his own safety, was offered by government assistance to emigrate to the colonies, but refused to leave England. He took work in a factory in the south, but left that job after he was recognised by a man he had known at Rotherham. He then relocated again with government help. What happened to him after that is not known.

Holberry has not been forgotten by his adopted city. His grave in the General Cemetery is a tourist attraction and in the Peace Gardens close by the present Town Hall is a commemorative plaque. One likes to think that the man, who was imprisoned for planning to seize the Town Hall of his day, would appreciate the irony.

The Wardsend Cemetery Riot, 1862

In eighteenth and early nineteenth-century England the teaching and study of anatomy was hampered by the lack of bodies for dissection. The only legitimate source of supply was the gallows (by s 1 of the Murder Act, 1751 judges were given a discretion to order that the body of a convicted murderer be handed over for dissection after execution). But the number of convicts ordered to be dissected each year was far too small to meet the demands of the medical profession, which was driven to rely upon grave robbers to provide it with the supply of fresh corpses it required.

Although their medical schools had long made London and Edinburgh centres of 'the resurrection trade,' the evil was not confined to those cities but flourished wherever anatomy was taught.[31]

In the early 1820s, leading Sheffield surgeon, Hall Overend, opened a private school of anatomy in the town. This proved an immediate success and soon removed to larger premises in Church Street.[32] In February 1828, at a meeting at the Cutlers' Hall, the town's leading medical practitioners came out strongly in favour of establishing a Sheffield medical school.[33] Aided by generous donations from the Duke of Norfolk and the Town Trustees, the project quickly got off the ground. A site was purchased on the corner of Surrey Street and Arundel Street. The promoters also despatched a petition to parliament asking 'for the removal of the obstructions which prevented the study of anatomy.' By July 1829 building work was completed and the school opened its doors for the first time.[34]

It had been hoped that Overend would throw in his lot with the new institution but, after initially showing interest, he fell out with the promoters and decided to carry on teaching from his own premises. Like most teachers of anatomy, he had, from the first, experienced great difficulty in obtaining corpses and was generally believed to be behind much of the grave robbing which took place in the Sheffield area. An incident, in relation to which

---

[31] The first provincial school of anatomy, outside Oxford and Cambridge, was founded in 1814 in Bridge Street, Manchester.
[32] To the rear of the premises was a small museum and it was here that Overend and his son, William, did their teaching.
[33] The resolution was for the establishment of 'an institution [comprising] a library, a museum, a lecture room and a room for dissection' (A. Jackson, Scraps from Medical History of Sheffield, Pawson & Brailsford, Sheffield, 1883, p. 13).
[34] It remained the home of medical education in Sheffield until 1888 when it moved to new premises in Leopold Street.

he was widely suspected, is described by Harold Armitage in his book *Chantrey Land*

> *In Norton there was a woman whose every joint was double, that is it would bend both backwards and forwards with equal ease. Her name was Susan Wilcockson, she lived at Cliffe Field and the doctors regarded her with curiosity. At her funeral Mr Herbert Rhodes of the post office, who, more than eighty years of age, has survived to our own time, remembers that a conveyance was passing to and fro while the service was being read and two hours after it had been buried the body had gone. Mr Rhodes recalls that 60 or 70 years ago it was usual for the friends of those who had been buried to spend several nights in the church-yard to keep watch and ward over the graves of the departed.*[35]

The founders of the Sheffield school were not the only persons pressing for the law to be altered. The disclosures in the Burke and Hare case in 1829[36] had not only shocked the public but made reform inevitable. It came in 1832 in the form of an Anatomy Act.

---

[35] Applebaum, Sheffield 1998 (reprint) at pp 95-96. Armitage adds 'There is an idea among Norton People that Mary Wilcockson's skeleton is now at the Sheffield medical school.' It would seem probable, however, that it ended up in the museum of the Sheffield General Infirmary (see W Smith Porter, *The Medical School in Sheffield 1828-1928*, J W Northend, Sheffield (1928), p 4 'Most of Mr Hall Overend's museum specimens passed ultimately into the hands of the Literary and Philosophical Society and of the Board of the Sheffield General Infirmary. In the museum of the latter institution there was preserved in a glass cabinet the skeleton of an undersized female adult, remarkable for rachitic deformation, which had formed part of Mr Overend's collection (he then proceeds to give an account of the acquisition of the body which tallies almost exactly with that given by Armitage). Grave robbing in South Yorkshire did not, however, start with Overend; in 1745 a watch house was built at the gates of St Nicholas church-yard, High Bradfield, with a view to preventing bodysnatching.

[36] Burke and Hare had made a rich living by murdering drunks and down-and-outs and selling their bodies to Robert Knox, an eminent Edinburgh surgeon (it is thought that they were responsible for at least 16 murders). They were caught in 1828. Burke was tried, convicted and executed. Hare saved his neck by turning King's evidence.

This provided that no person should practise anatomy, whether as teacher or student, without a Home Office licence; that the only bodies which could be received for dissection by anatomy schools were the unclaimed corpses of workhouse paupers and bodies given for dissection by executors or others in lawful possession;[37] and that anatomy schools should be subject to government inspection and control and should make quarterly returns to the Home Office of all dissections carried out.

Although the Act did much to stem the trade in dead bodies, it did not eliminate it entirely. Nor did it affect the suspicion with which medical schools and anatomists were viewed by the populace. Within weeks of its coming into force, there was rioting in Manchester when it was discovered that a local surgeon had, prior to burial, cut off the head of a boy who had died in hospital. The windows of the medical school were smashed and only the arrival of cavalry prevented even more extensive damage being done. In December 1833 a mob attacked the medical school at Cambridge in the mistaken belief that unlawful means of obtaining bodies were still being employed.[38]

In 1835 it was the turn of Overend's school to suffer.[39] On Sunday, January 25, the peace of Eyre Street, to which the school had recently removed, was shattered by the sound of a woman screaming. It was, in fact, the school caretaker's wife who was being beaten by her drunken husband. Her cries of 'murder' caused a crowd to gather and the rumour quickly spread that she

---

[37] Unless prohibited from so doing the deceased's will or by the surviving relatives.
[38] See B Bailey, *The Resurrection Men*, Macdonald, London, 1991, p. 159.
[39] For press reports of the riot, see *The Sheffield Independent*, January 31, 1835 and the *Sheffield Mercury* for the same date.

was being 'burked.' A handful of bystanders forced their way into the building, but were quickly arrested and the premises placed under police guard.

The following morning, the crowd which the incident had attracted having finally dispersed, the police withdrew.

At around 7 a.m. a mob broke into the school. Furniture, books, floorboards and, indeed, anything the looters could lay hands on was piled in the street and set on fire. When the fire brigade arrived, the firemen were stoned and forced to withdraw.

With his officers hopelessly outnumbered and completely unable to restore order, Raynor, the chief constable, sent for dragoons from the Philadelphia Barracks. Still the crowd did not disperse and the Riot Act had to be read.[40] For several hours, the troops and two of the town's magistrates rode back and forth along Eyre Street and the adjoining streets, urging people to leave. But it was a slow business. By now, sightseers were arriving in numbers and some of the crowd were still out for trouble. A fresh street fire was started but quickly put out. In the early evening, the Surrey Street medical school was stoned and a rush made upon Overend's house in Church Street. The attackers were beaten off, although not before most of the ground floor windows of the medical school had been put it.

The riot signalled the end for Overend's school, which never reopened. It also led to the prosecution for public nuisance of a printer who, on the Monday, had put out a broadsheet full of untruths entitled 'The New DISSECTING HOUSE

---

[40] Failure by rioters to disperse within an hour after the reading of the Act was a felony.

DISSECTED.' The *Sheffield Independent* in an editorial commented

> *'The popular prejudices which have produced this event can only be classed with those which, centuries ago, caused the prosecution of old women as witches.'*[41]

Although the Surrey Street medical school came through the 1835 riot largely unscathed, popular feeling in the town against dissection remained strong and in 1862 there was another riot, this time at Wardsend cemetery.[42]

In June, 1862 a man, named Dixon, who lived above the coach house in the cemetery and who had had a falling out with Isaac Howard, the sexton, complained to the police that Howard had been selling bodies to the medical school. Although Dixon was of bad character (he had served prison sentences for dishonesty) and had an obvious motive for making false accusations, it looked as though he might actually be telling the truth. He had alleged that there was a pit in the cemetery in which disinterred bodies and coffins were put once they had served the sexton's purpose, and not only was there such a pit but, when the boarding was removed from it, inside were found some twenty or so children's coffins, a quantity of human remains and an open

---

[41] *The Sheffield Independent*, January 31, 1835.
[42] With the closing in 1855-56 of most of the Town's burial grounds, suburban cemeteries began to make their appearance. Wardsend lay within the parish of St Philip's and when, in 1857, the parish church-yard was closed for interments, the vicar, the Rev Livesey, had, at his own expense, bought five acres of land at the foot of Old Park Wood which he laid out as a new parish cemetery. Consecrated in 1859 the cemetery had the unique distinction of having a railway line running through it. For the riot and the subsequent proceedings before the Sheffield magistrates, see *The Times*, June 5, 7, 9, 10, 14, 23 & 24, 1862 and *The Sheffield Independent*, June 5, 7, 10, 13, 17, 21, 24, 1862.

deal box containing a dissected body. Also, it was clear from the plate on one of the coffins that it was that of a child, who had originally been buried in another part of the cemetery.

When word of this got abroad, worried parents descended on the cemetery anxious to discover whether the graves of their dead children had been disturbed, some even going so far as to break open graves to satisfy themselves that the coffin was still there and intact. When a mother claimed that she recognised one of the bodies in the pit as that of her child the news spread like wildfire. A mob set off in search of Howard. Not finding him, they turned his wife out of her house and fired the building.

Fearing that the medical school might be the next place to be attacked the police placed a guard around it. [43]

On June 7, Howard gave himself up to the police. The next day he was brought before the town's magistrates charged with disinterring dead bodies and, in due course, committed for trial.

Police inquiries at the medical school established that the dissected corpse found in the pit was that of Joseph Gretorex. He had died in the workhouse on March 8. Two days later his body was removed to the medical school. Wardsend was the cemetery which the school used for the disposal of dissected corpses, and, on April 3, Howard was notified that there was a body for burial.

---

[43] See W. Smith Porter, op. cit., p. 13 '[after] the discovery of these irregularities at Wardsend Cemetery, [threats] were levelled against the Medical school in Surrey Street, and it was feared that the mob might repeat the occurrence of 1835, when the Eyre Street school was sacked and destroyed. In 1862 my father was in practice in Leader House, at the junction of Surrey Street and Eyre Street ... I well remember being taken out of bed at an hour which seemed to be in the middle of the night and conveyed in a cab to my grandfather's residence, Dam House, quite out in the country. What fixed the occasion in my memory was the spectacle of a police picket in front of the medical school and watch fires burning in the middle of the street. I believe the Medical School was guarded for two or three days until popular feeling had become less acute.'

He called to collect it on April 12, put it in the deal box and took it away on a wheelbarrow. On May 12, he dumped it in the pit.

When the police inspected the cemetery burial register they found the following entry in the handwriting of the Rev Livesey, the vicar of St Phillip's

BURIALS IN THE PARISH OF ST PHILIP, SHEFFIELD, IN THE COUNTY OF YORK, IN THE YEAR 1862

Name	Abode	When buried	Age	By whom the ceremony was performed
Joseph Gretorex	Medical School	April 3	56 years	John Livesey

The entry was plainly false in two respects: the date of burial was wrong (the body was still at the medical school on April 3); also, as inquiry of the gravediggers at the cemetery established and as the vicar was himself to admit, no burial service had ever been performed. Nor was it the only false document which the vicar had signed; he had also issued a false burial certificate. On May 23 he was committed for trial by the Sheffield magistrates on a charge of making a false entry in a burial register.

The cases of Howard and Livesey came on for trial at York Assizes on July 24, 1862 before Mr Justice Mellor.[44] The vicar was tried first, Howard being one of the witnesses called against him. A letter, which the vicar had written to the *Sheffield Daily*

---

[44] Mr Price QC and Mr Hannay prosecuted the vicar who was defended by Mr Bliss QC and Mr Blanshard. Mr Hannay and the Hon F.S Wortley prosecuted Howard, who was defended by Mr Maule and Mr Kyd. For reports of the trials see *The Times*, July 26, 1862 and the *Sheffield Independent*, July 25, 1862.

Telegraph, was put in by the prosecution. In it he had claimed that he had made the entry in the register, relying on information supplied by Howard and that Howard had misinformed him of the date of the burial. This was what his counsel urged the jury to find. That was credible enough but what of the words '[ceremony performed by] John Livesey'? How were they to be explained? What was meant by that, said counsel, was that the interment was made in the vicar's own cemetery in consecrated ground, namely in the catacomb,[45] where such bodies were usually placed. It was ingenious but it did not wash. After just over half an hour's retirement the jury returned with a verdict of guilty.

The vicar was taken below and Howard took his place in the dock. The indictment against him charged him with disinterring two named children whose coffins had been found in the pit. That he had dug up their bodies was clearly proved but the question on everyone's lips was why. The explanation offered by his counsel was one which the vicar had given to the press shortly after the riot: in order to provide space for further burials, he had adopted the practice of digging up the coffins of children which lay in unpurchased graves and reburying them in the pit. The judge in his summing up told the jury that the explanation offered provided no justification in law for what had been done.

> *'if the place was overcrowded the remedy was by increasing the size of the grounds not by removing bodies from the places in which they had been solemnly interred. If*

---

[45] The catacomb was the name counsel chose to give to the boarded up pit.

> *[counsel's] plea was right a man who was buried last week might be removed this week, on the plea that the exigencies of the [burial] ground required it.'*

The jury immediately convicted without leaving their box.

The vicar having been brought up from the cells, Mr Justice Mellor sentenced both men to imprisonment; the Rev Livesey received three weeks, Howard three months. For the vicar, however, the affair was to have a happy ending. After his conviction, his parishioners, who had been calling for his removal at the time of the riot, now came to his aid pressing successfully for him to be granted a free pardon.[46] He remained vicar of St Philips until his death on August 10, 1870.[47] Two years after his death the road leading to the cemetery was renamed Livesey Street.[48]

The Wardsend riot was the last resurrection scandal of the nineteenth century and, although the medical school was cleared of any charge that it was dealing in corpses, the fact that Gretorex's dissected body (and probably many others before) had, in plain breach of the Anatomy Act, been removed from the school in a box and then unceremoniously dumped in a pit, reflected little credit upon either school or cemetery. It certainly did little to advance the cause of anatomy in the town but rather

---

[46] In November, 1862 Howard was awarded £200 compensation by the Strafforth and Tickhill hundred for the damage to his home and furniture (*The Times*, November 10, 1862).
[47] For his obituary, see *The Sheffield Independent*, August 12, 1870.
[48] It had formerly been called Cemetery Road (see P. Harvey, *The Street Names of Sheffield*, Sheaf Publishing, Sheffield, 2001, p. 90).

served to confirm the prejudices of those, of whom there were many in 1860s Sheffield, opposed to anatomical dissection.[49]

Sheffield Prisons

Sheffield has never had and, even today, still does not have, a criminal prison.[50] In the eighteenth and nineteenth centuries it did, however, have two debtors' gaols. The gaols were those of the Ecclesall and Sheffield courts of requests. These courts, created in 1756 by local Act of Parliament, sat to hear claims for sums of 40s or less and had power to imprison debtors who failed to satisfy judgments given against them. Until 1808 the longest term for which a debtor could be committed for non-payment was three months. In 1808, a second local Act increased the financial limit on the courts' jurisdiction to £5, and, at the same time, placed tighter restrictions on their power to imprison for debt. The maximum term for which a debtor could be committed was to depend upon the amount of the judgment debt:

> *up to 20 days for a debt of 20 shillings or under;*
> *up to 40 days for a debt between 20 and 40 shillings;*
> *up to 60 days for a debt between 40 shillings and £3;*
> *up to 80 days for a debt between £3 and £4 and*
> *up to 100 days for debts over £4.*

---

[49] Several witnesses at the trial had spoken of the strong feeling which had long prevailed in the town against dissection.
[50] The principal reason for this is that Sheffield only became an assize town very late in the day (1955) and it was in assize towns that the main criminal gaols were situated. It did, however, have cells beneath the Town Hall and later police cells where those arrested could be held until they could be brought before the magistrates.

At one time a debtor, who had served the term for which he had been committed, could be further detained until he had paid off the gaoler's fees, but in 1816 Bennet's Act changed this rule: henceforth no prisoner, whether for crime or debt, was to be detained on account of jailer's fees.

In the eighteenth century, the prison of the Sheffield court of requests was situated in Pudding Lane (now King Street). That of the Ecclesall court, known as Little Sheffield, stood at the corner of Bishop Street and Tudor Street near Moorfoot.

The King Street gaol had a very bad reputation. When Howard, the prison reformer, visited it in the 1770s he found it 'filthy beyond description,' with men and women huddled together in dark, evil smelling, small cells, all sleeping in beds made up on the stone floor. It stood on the north side of the street next to the *Royal Oak* public house, for which the gaoler held the licence.

Unlike those imprisoned for crime, debtors had no right to the 'county bread' or to poor relief. Under a statute of 1756 (Lord's Act), a creditor who had his debtor incarcerated was required to allow him 4d a day for his maintenance, but in practice the provision proved a dead letter.[51] At King Street, debtors were, however, allowed to carry on their trades and a visitor to the prison would commonly hear 'cutlers and file cutters

---

[51] S & B Webb, *English Prisons under Local Government*, Longmans & Green, London 1922, p 12. By the nineteenth century debtors who had no other means of support could apply to the poor law authorities for the 'bread dole.' (an application by a Scotland Street prisoner for bread dole dating from the 1830s has survived – see *Sheffield Weekly Independent*, September 8, 1917; there is a copy of it on *Picture Sheffield*).

hammering away as if they were in their own shops.'[52] This, and the charity of friends, was how inmates supported themselves, supplemented by what they got by begging: from a first floor window was hung a tin, and out of a ground floor window an inmate would hold a box to solicit coins from passers-by.[53]

On first entering the prison, a newcomer would be required to pay garnish[54]: 2/6 for those in 'high court,' the better part of the prison, 1s 2d for those in 'low court.' There were also gaol fees to pay, 25s or 6d depending on the accommodation occupied.

In 1791, the prison and the gaoler's house were attacked during the Broomhall riots and the gates broken open, but the prisoners, no doubt to the puzzlement of the rioters, refused to leave.[55]

A visitor to the prison in 1802 found that conditions were marginally better than in Howard's time. Prisoners who fell ill were now attended by the surgeon to the poor law overseers, but there was no chaplain and no provision for religious worship.

In 1818 the King Street building was pulled down and the jailer and inmates transferred to a new gaol in Scotland Street. The new prison, a converted merchant's warehouse, was quickly given the nickname 'Edinburgh Castle.' Its walls were extremely thick and the cells badly lit. To the rear was a small parade ground where the prisoners could be mustered. A report from 1836 gives an insight into conditions there:

---

[52] R E Leader, *Reminiscences of Old Sheffield*, Leader & Sons, Sheffield, 1876, p 89.
[53] Ibid., p. 90.
[54] A sum to be spent by the other inmates on drink; those who could not or would not pay were stripped and made to run the gauntlet.
[55] For an account of the riot, see D. Bentley, *The Sheffield Hanged*, ALD Sheffield, 2002, pp. 52-63.

> *There are no rules for the government of the prison. The keeper has applied to the court upon many occasions but they have declined interfering, doubting their power to do so. The prisoners make rules for themselves: they collect garnish and they impose fines and penalties. One punishment is walking through the yard with a bell round the neck. He has lately set aside a room for refractory prisoners but it is of no use. There is a great deal of singing and noise but not so much as there was before the reduction of the quantity of liquor. [Included amongst the rules made and enforced by the prisoners are the following:]*
>
> *At the coming in of any bird he shall pay 2s 6d to the garnish master, or have his hat and coat taken for security; and, if not paid in seven days, the coals of the room will be stopped until it is paid. But should any bird go under 12 hours he will have 1s 3d returned and, at the coming in of a woman, she shall pay 1s 3d garnish, or have her bonnet and shawl taken for security until the same shall be paid.*
> *At the coming in of a bird the captain or substitute will attend or be fined 2s for neglect of duty.*
> *Any man coming in shall commence Nancy next morning at 9 o'clock.*
> *The office of cleaning the room is imposed upon the youngest prisoner.*
> *All schedulers shall pay 2s 6d foot ale[56] and 14d room money. No other man will pay foot ale. The scheduler to pay foot ale and room money to the room he was allotted to.*
> *Any person found 'ghosting' a new bird shall be fined 2s 6d.[57]*
>
> *The keeper was appointed in 1832 by His Grace the Duke of Norfolk. He is paid by fees allowed and inserted in the 48 G III; their gross amount has been about £1,000. He pays the expenses of the office. The receipts vary and the expenses also in proportion. He states that his clear income from this source to be from £600 to £700, with residence. He keeps one turnkey, who resides in the prison, and to whom he pays a salary of £52 p.a.[58]*

In 1825 the Home Office asked for information about the Ecclesall prison. It was told that the gaol comprised

> *a court room 7 yards wide by 8 yards long and a room to receive and pay money 4 yards square; beneath these lie three prison rooms, one measuring 6 yards wide by 7 yards long, the other two 3 yards*

---

[56] Foot ale – an old custom amongst miners when a man first enters into work to pay his first day's wages for ale (*Oxford English Dictionary* citing Hooson's *Miners' Dictionary*)
[57] *Quaere* taking advantage of a new inmate.
[58] *South Yorkshire Notes and Queries*, W C Leng, Sheffield, vol 2 (1900), p. 188.

by 7 yards. Outside is an exercise yard which is 35 yards round with a pump which often runs dry in the summer. There is also a gaoler's house consisting of two lower rooms and three chambers.[59]

In 1844, imprisonment for debt under £20 having been abolished by statute,[60] the 80 prisoners in the Scotland Street gaol and the nine in Little London were freed and the gaols closed.[61]

In 1851 the town council petitioned the Home Office to use the Scotland Street premises for county court commitments, instead of sending defaulters to York. This, however, was refused, it being decided to send prisoners to Halifax.[62]

In the 1870s the building was sold and occupied until 1919 first by an oyster dealer, and then by a sweet merchant, with the upper stories let out as offices.[63] In 1923 it was pulled down. When it was demolished two heavy, thick and iron-studded doors were discovered.

After its closure, the Little Sheffield prison was also sold off. It became first a warehouse then a grinding shop, known as the Old Jail Wheel.[64] It was still being so used as late as 1944.[65] But it had lost none of its menace 'A great ugly building 30 feet high, the shadow of which seems to shut out the light and cast a

---

[59] G F Usherwood, *Ecclesall Debtors' Gaol*, Transactions of the Hunter Archaeological Society, vol 5, p. 131.
[60] Execution Act, 1844 (7 & 8 Vict., c 96). In 1833 the overseers of the rural parishes of Sheffield had petitioned for the abolition of the practice of imprisoning people for debts under £5, on the ground that the cost to them of maintaining such prisoners and their families exceeded the amount of the debts for which they were committed. (Sheffield Local Studies Library, *Newspaper Cuttings Relating to Sheffield*, 942.74 SF, vol 4, p 40).
[61] J M Furness, *Fifty Years of Municipal Records*, Wm Townsend & Son, Sheffield, 1893, p 80.
[62] Ibid., p 97.
[63] See White's *Directory of Sheffield* for the years 1879 to 1923.
[64] *Sheffield Telegraph*, January 8, 1934 (letter); in *The Transactions of the Hunter Archaeological Society*, vol 6, at p 136 is a photograph of an envelope dated May 16, 1870 addressed to the Old Jail Wheel.
[65] *The Star*, March 4, 1944.

gloom over the surrounding houses' is how a correspondent of a Sheffield newspaper described it in 1887.[66]

When in November 1939 an air raid shelter was built beneath the *Royal Oak* in King Street, remains of the old prison were found:

> 'Off a 100' long passage, 20' high and 20' wide are a dozen cubicles which are believed to be cells. In the old stone walls are small recesses where chains could have been fixed.[67]

Today, the debtors' prisons are but a memory. Those committed to custody by the local civil courts for contempt now serve their sentences in Armley or one of the other Yorkshire prisons. The only cells, which now remain in Sheffield, are those in its court buildings and police stations – a situation which is unique for a city of its size.

Derbyshire's Lord Chief Justice[68]

Stoney Middleton Hall[69] may not be one of Derbyshire's most impressive country houses, but it has this distinction: it was from 1830 to 1854 the favourite retreat of England's Lord Chief Justice, Lord Denman.

---

[66] *Sheffield Telegraph*, December 14, 1938.
[67] *Sheffield Telegraph*, November 1, 1939
[68] See generally Sir J Arnould, *Memoirs of Thomas, First Lord Denman*, Longman & Green, London, 1871, DNB, and Holdsworth, *A History of English Law*, Methuen & Co., London 1965, vol xv, 395-405.
[69] The Hall is a twin gabled building dating from around 1600. According to C Daniel, *Stoney Middleton, a Village Lord Denman Knew*, Derbyshire Countryside, vol. 20, no 3, p 64 it had at one time been the village parsonage.

The Denmans were originally a Nottinghamshire family but in the early eighteenth century, John Denman moved to Bakewell where he set up practice as a surgeon.[70] His two sons Joseph and Thomas followed him into the medical profession.[71]

Joseph stayed put in Bakewell and in 1761 married Elizabeth Finney, a lady of property whose landed assets included the small Stoney Middleton estate. With the passage of the years his reputation grew; he practised a good deal at Buxton during the season, and even wrote a treatise on *Buxton Water.* In his later years he was a frequent visitor to Chatsworth, being a great favourite of the third Duke.

His younger brother, Thomas, had to move to London to get his start.[72] His first appointment was as an apothecary at St George's Hospital but he then joined the navy, attaining the rank of ship's surgeon. After taking a doctorate in medicine at Aberdeen University, he finally set up in private practice, first at Winchester then in London specialising in midwifery. He quickly earned for himself the reputation of one of the up-and-coming men in the field and, in 1769, was appointed Surgeon Accoucheur to the Middlesex Hospital. By then he was married[73] and on July 23, 1779, at his town house at 30, Golden Square, his son Thomas, the future Lord Denman, was born.[74]

---

[70] He practised from premises in Bridge Street. The DNB says he was an apothecary not a doctor.
[71] Both were educated at Bakewell Grammar School.
[72] He is said to have gone up to London in 21st year with £75 in his pocket, £50 bequeathed by his grandfather and £25 as his share of what is father was supposed to have been worth at the time of his death
[73] His wife, who was 14 years his junior, was the daughter of Alexander Brewer, a Scottish accoutrement maker
[74] He was in fact their third child. The couple also had twin girls born November 1, 1770.

There must have been many who expected that the boy would follow his father's profession but it was not to be. On leaving Cambridge, breaking with family tradition, he decided to go in for the law. It was to prove a wise decision. Called to the bar in 1806 he was almost immediately successful.[75] In 1814 he appeared for defendants indicted with Lord Cochrane for a huge Stock Exchange fraud and in 1816 was briefed in a Luddite trial. The following year 'he made his name by the ability with which he defended Brandreth and two of his companions on a charge of treason.'[76]

In 1819 he was elected MP for the close borough of Wareham (Dorset). In parliament, he supported proposals for reform of the criminal law and the abolition of the slave trade. He was especially prominent in the campaign to abolish the death penalty in cases of forgery and 'fearless in denouncing jobbery corruption and any species of oppression at home or abroad.'[77]

The case which brought him to general public notice was the trial of Queen Caroline in 1820, for whom he and Henry Brougham appeared as counsel.[78] His masterful speech at the bar of the House of Lords played no small part in persuading their lordships to throw out the bill of pains and penalties which the government had brought against her.[79] But it was a success

---

[75] In 1804 he had married Theodosia Vevers, the daughter of the Rev Vevers of Saxby near Melton Mowbray. With his family ties, it was hardly surprising that the circuit which had he chosen to join after his call to the bar was the Midland. He appears to have attracted work almost immediately. In 1807 he wrote to his wife that he had had a 'prosperous sessions' and in a letter of 1808 spoke of having had four briefs at the Derby Spring Assizes (Arnould, op. cit., i, 63).
[76] Holdsworth, op. cit., xv, p 396.
[77] Arnould, op. cit., i, 121.
[78] The Queen had appointed Brougham as her attorney-general and Denman as her solicitor-general.
[79] The purpose of the bill was to grant the King a divorce on the ground of the Queen's adultery.

bought at a price – the bitter enmity of George IV, who took an allusion by Denman to Nero as a reference to himself. The King gained his revenge by refusing to appoint Denman King's Counsel.

But, if the king was hostile, the city of London was not and in 1822 he was elected Common Serjeant of London, a part time judicial office, which carried a salary of £1000 p.a.[80] But the fact that he was being kept out of silk not only irked him, but was also professionally damaging. In 1827, at a dinner at the Fishmongers' Hall, he referred publicly to his exclusion. The following year, having learned from Lord Chancellor Lyndhurst the reason for the King's antipathy, he assured him that no imputation against His Majesty's character had ever been intended and he asked Lyndhurst to intercede on his behalf. When he declined Denman enlisted the help of the Duke of Wellington. The Duke, at length, persuaded the king to relent but only with the greatest difficulty. 'By God it was the toughest job I ever had,' he remarked afterwards.[81]

Throughout his life Denman had family ties with Derbyshire. In his youth and, as an undergraduate, he had visited Stoney Middleton and, on the death of his uncle Thomas in 1812, he inherited the Hall. When in 1830[82] the tenant, who had been in occupation of the Hall at his uncle's death, moved out, Denman resolved to make it his summer residence. The Hall at this time was 'a rough old place: an old fashioned grange or small manor

---

[80] And fees for city business which varied between £150 and £400 p.a.
[81] Arnould, op. cit., i, 281; Denman was appointed KC in 1828.
[82] 1830 also saw Denman, who had been out of parliament since 1826, elected MP for Nottingham.

house with ill-arranged rooms and whitewashed walls.'[83] Nonetheless, Denman was captivated by it and, during the succeeding years, he devoted a huge amount of time and energy to improving the house and its gardens.[84] Indeed, the work became one of the loves of his life. To quote his sister, Mrs Baillie, 'he engaged himself completely, entering with delight onto the improvement of his little domain, planting and transplanting trees with his own hand and labouring with as much eagerness and interest as though this land had been the sole occupation of his life.'[85] One of the works which he undertook was the restoration of what was believed to be a Roman bath lying behind the Hall.[86]

By the time he took up occupation of the Hall, Denman's star was in the ascendant. In 1830 he was appointed Attorney General. The Lord Chief Justiceship followed two years later and in 1833 he was granted a peerage (he took the title Lord Denman

---

[83] 'Mr Radford the late tenant had edged [the whitewashed walls] with a deep border of black out of respect for the memory of his deceased wife. Lord Wensleydale used to say of the Hall 'even in its improved state… that Denman must be very fond of ancestral property to like such a house' (Arnould, op. cit., I, 384).

[84] On October 7, 1832 he wrote to his mother 'We ride daily and we have visited more of the beautiful scenes of this varied county than I ever saw before. We have nearly done with workmen about the house which has been made very convenient; but some small improvements are projected in the garden for another year. We have excellent neighbours and more going out than I could desire.' (Arnould, op cit., i, 386).

[85] In July 1840 he wrote to his friend, Merivale, telling him in triumph that he had been able to accomplish the journey from Portland Place to Stoney Middleton in ten hours. In another letter from around the same time he wrote ' My holiday here began on the 8th, the music of the axe has been sounding ever since.' (Arnould, op. cit., ii, 227 and 109).

[86] Denman was, it seems, very popular in the village – see Daniel, op. cit., p 64 :
'For many years [after his death] the [villagers] would entertain their children and grandchildren with the stories they remembered. One [concerned] a tenant who accosted his lordship in the street, upbraiding him because of the state of disrepair into which his cottage had fallen and threatening to leave if the required repairs were not carried out forthwith. The great lawyer listened to his indignant tenant with surprise and some amusement, because he had hitherto been unaware that the cottage was his property. A subsequent examination of the rent book confirmed the tenant's claim, and also disclosed that he had not paid any rent for almost seven years.'

of Dovedale).[87] In office he presided over many high profile cases, including *Stockdale v Hansard* and the trial of Lord Cardigan.[88] In the upper House he supported the cause of law reform and fought unsparingly for the abolition of the slave trade.

In 1849, he suffered two strokes but refused all urgings to retire. Unable to face the prospect of being succeeded by Lord Campbell, for whom he entertained a strong dislike, he held on to office for as long as he could, only resigning in February 1850. He retired to Stoney Middleton and there his health gradually improved.[89] In 1852, however, his wife died. Soon afterwards, he had a further stroke which left him partly paralysed. After treatment, he again returned to the Hall where he was cared for by his daughter, Mrs Hodgson. In Spring 1854, he left Stoney Middleton for the last time and went to live with his eldest son at Stoke Albany, Northamptonshire where he died on September 22, 1854. He is buried in the churchyard there.[90]

---

[87] He had been on a walking tour in Dovedale in 1798 and had never forgotten the area (Arnould, op. cit., i, p. 20).

[88] *Stockdale v Hansard* (1839) 9 Ad & E 1 concerned parliamentary privilege; Cardigan was tried by the House of Lords for attempted murder and acquitted on a technicality.

[89] On December 22 in a letter to Coleridge J he writes of a 'drive and visit to monster lily at Chatsworth covering a tank 20 feet square.'(Arnould, op. cit., vol ii, 276).

[90] Denman left five sons: Thomas, Joseph, Richard, George and Lewis and six daughters.

Thomas, the 2nd Lord Denman, (b 1805) continued to live at the Hall and is still remembered in the village as a benevolent, if eccentric, squire who bred black pigs. He gave the village a reading room. On the death of his wife he erected a monument to her on an area of moorland known as Denman's Moor. 'It is a simple but sturdy cross hewn from ... millstone grit...The only inscription it bears is 'He who believes in Me shall have everlasting life' Daniel, op. cit. p. 65.

Joseph (b 1810) joined the navy rising to the rank of Vice-Admiral; in 1840, while serving off the African coast, he set fire to a slave house belonging to a Spaniard and freed the slaves. In 1848 the Spaniard sued him for trespass but, since the act complained of took place outside the jurisdiction, Denman was able successfully to plead 'Act of State' (*Buron v Denman* (1848) 2 Ex 167).

Richard (b 1814) was called to the bar and became Clerk of Assize for the Home Circuit

George (b 1819) was called to the bar in 1846; QC 1861; MP for Tiverton, 1859-72 when he was made a judge of the Court of the Common Pleas and then (after 1873) a High Court judge.

Lewis (b 1821) became a clergyman. Denman's second daughter, Elizabeth (b 1807) married his lifelong friend the Rev Francis Hodgson, then vicar of Bakewell and Edensor; later Archdeacon of Derbyshire and Provost of Eton.

The Padley Martyrs

On the morning of July 12, 1588, with England under threat of invasion by Spain,[91] a band of armed men led by the Lord Lieutenant of Derbyshire, George, Earl of Shrewsbury, descended on Padley Manor near Grindleford.[92] Their purpose was to arrest and intern John Fitzherbert,[93] the tenant of the hall and a member of one the county's most prominent Catholic families.[94] The manor had long been a missionary haven for catholic priests and when it was searched two English born seminary priests, Nicholas Garlick and Robert Ludlam were found hiding in a chimney.[95] For them capture was equivalent to a death sentence, a statute of 1585 having made it treason for any Catholic priest ordained abroad to come into, be or remain in any part of the realm.[96] Together with

---

[91] The government feared and the Spanish were confident that an invasion would be supported by a general rising of English Catholics (J B Black, *The Reign of Elizabeth*, Oxford History of England, p 393). In December, 1587 the Privy Council had issued instructions to the Lords Lieutenant of counties to arrest the most obstinate Catholic recusants in their areas and to place those 'of value but not so obstinate' in the custody of an Anglican clergyman or other 'gentleman well affected.' (*Padley, A Pilgrim's Guide*, Diocese of Nottingham 1978, p. 6).

[92] The manor house, which dated from about 1400, stood on the north bank of the river Derwent a mile above Grindleford.

[93] Shrewsbury had sent men to Padley to arrest John Fizherbert at Candlemas, 1587 but he was not there. On July 12 he was acting on a tip off from John's youngest son, Thomas, who hoped by his treachery to obtain a grant from the Crown of his father's lands.

[94] The Fitzherberts were an old Derbyshire family with estates at Norbury, Tissington and Somersal. Buried is Norbury Church is their most distinguished son, Sir Anthony Fitzherbert (1514-1538); a judge of the Common Pleas under Henry VIII and a celebrated legal scholar. Padley manor had passed into their hands following the marriage in the mid sixteenth century of Sir Thomas Fitzherbert to Ann Eyre, the sole Padley heiress. Thomas was imprisoned at Derby in 1559 for recusancy, then in a succession of London gaols, the Fleet, Lambeth and finally the Tower, where he died on December 1, 1591 aged seventy-four.

[95] Natives of Derbyshire, both had in the early 1580s trained for the priesthood at the English College at Rheims and, following their ordination, had returned to England to minister to the Catholic faithful. Garlick had been caught and expelled in 1585 but had returned knowing that if he was arrested again his life would be forfeit.

[96] The statute made it a felony punishable by death for any person to 'receive, relieve or comfort' such a priest.

Fitzherbert, two of his children and ten of his male servants they were despatched to Derby gaol.[97]

Eleven days later the priests stood trial for treason. Convicted in short order they were sentenced to be hung drawn and quartered.[98] They went to the scaffold with John Simpson, a fellow priest who had been convicted the previous January.[99] While awaiting trial they had stiffened Simpson's resolve and also converted to Catholicism a woman under sentence of death for murder.

On July 24, they, Simpson and the murderess were taken to St Mary's Bridge, Derby[100] for execution. Known to posterity as the Padley martyrs they died bravely. As they were being dragged to the scaffold on hurdles, a man in the crowd reminded Garlick that the two of them had often gone shooting together when they were younger. 'True,' came the reply, "but now I am to shoot such a shot as I have never shot in my life." On arrival at the bridge the cauldron, which was to be used to boil their entrails once they had been disembowelled, was not ready and Garlick took advantage of the delay to preach to the crowd urging them to

---

[97] Two of John's daughters were placed in the custody of the Anglican rectors of Aston and Weston upon Trent. His son Anthony and his daughter Maud were imprisoned in Derby gaol for three years. John himself was tried and sentenced to death but the sentence was never carried out; instead he was kept in Derby prison for two years and then sent to the Fleet prison in London where he died in November 1590 (it is said his reprieve from the death sentence cost his son in law Thomas Eyre £10,000 in bribes, the money being raised principally by the sale of Thomas's manor at Whittington). Padley manor itself escheated to the Crown.

[98] The form of the death sentence on male traitors at this period was 'Thou shalt be had from hence to the place whence thou didst come, and drawn [from thence] upon an hurdle to the place of execution, and there to be hanged and let down alive, and thy privy members cut off and thy entrails taken out and burned in thy sight; then thy head shall be cut off and thy body divided into four quarters to be disposed of at Her Majesty's pleasure.' (Cobbett & Howell, *State Trials*).

[99] Simpson, a native of Sheffield, had converted to Catholicism for which he had been imprisoned in York Castle. He trained as a priest at the Douai college in France and following his ordination returned to England to pursue his calling. It is said that prior to Garlick and Ludlam joining him he had been contemplating converting to Anglicanism to save his neck.

[100] The bridge was only a little distance from the county gaol in the Corn Market.

have a care for their souls. When all was ready he kissed the ladder before climbing to take the rope. Cut down while still conscious he was then disembowelled and quickly died. Simpson was the next to suffer. Ludlam watched the proceedings with a smile on his face and, while standing on the gallows ladder, cried out as if in ecstasy *'Venite benedicti dei.'*[101] After execution all three were beheaded and their bodies quartered, the heads were placed on spikes of the bridge, and their quarters exhibited at sites in the town.[102] It was a fate which befell nearly a score of other Catholic priests in Armada year.

Of Padley manor all that survives is a gatehouse.[103] This was purchased by the Catholic Diocese of Nottingham in 1933 and converted into a chapel. Every year on the Thursday nearest to July 12th a pilgrimage and service takes place there around an open air altar.

Emily Swann [104]

Ninety-four prisoners were executed at Armley gaol during the 101 years that it was a hanging prison. Of these one was a woman. She was Emily Swan from Wombwell, the first South Yorkshire woman to be hanged since Mary Thorpe in March,

---

[101] *Come blessed of God.* The murderess was executed on the same gallows as the priests but not cut down until she was dead.
[102] They were removed under cover of darkness by sympathisers and buried secretly. There is a legend that Garlick's head lies buried in Tideswell churchyard (before he became a priest he had been a schoolmaster at Tideswell for seven years).
[103] It owes its survival to the fact that, after the manor fell into decay, it had been used as a barn.
[104] See *Sheffield Independent.,* June 8, 10, August 6, 7, Dec 10, 1903; *Sheffield Telegraph* June 8, 10, 11, August 6, 7 & 19; December 10, 30, 1903; *The Star*, December 29, 1903; *The Times*, December 10, 1903; John Ellis, *Diary of a Hangman*, Forum Press London, 1996.

1800.[105] She was executed on December 29, 1903 together with her lover, John Gallagher. It was the only double hanging involving a man and a woman in the twentieth century.[106]

Gallagher came originally from Middlesbrough. After being discharged from the West Yorkshire Regiment for misconduct, he had ended up in Wombwell, where he obtained work as a miner at Mitchell Main colliery, and lodgings with William Swann and his family. Soon after moving in to the Swanns' home in Alma Court, George Square he became Emily's lover. That he was attracted to her at all was surprising. Twelve years his senior, the mother of eleven children and well past the bloom of youth, Emily was certainly no beauty. 'A little, stumpy, round-faced woman, only 4'10" tall and 122 lb in weight' was hangman Ellis's unflattering description. One thing which they did have in common, however, was a liking for drink. It was not the only characteristic they shared: both had a violent streak, Emily having in the past served a prison sentence for assault.

It was not long before William Swann found out what his wife and lodger were up to and, on three occasions, he ordered Gallagher out of the house. The third time Gallagher left but he did not go far, taking fresh lodgings across the street at the home of Mary Ann Ward. He continued to see Emily after he had

---

[105] For an account of Mary Thorpe's case see D.Bentley, *The Sheffield Hanged*, ALD, Sheffield, 2002, pp, 73-75.

[106] In 1923 Frederick Bywaters and Edith Thompson, convicted of the murder of the latter's husband, were executed at different prisons. In the eighteenth and nineteenth centuries men and women were often executed together (e.g. in 1800 Sheffield murderess, Mary Thorpe, was hanged alongside Michael Simpson). Same sex double executions remained common in the twentieth century; there being 55 such executions of male murderers (the last was that of Chrimes and Gilbert at Pentonville in 1954) and one double female execution (that of Sachs and Walters in 1903).

moved out, sleeping with her at least three times a week when her husband was working nights.[107] During daylight hours the couple were often seen out walking together, with Gallagher with his arm round Emily's waist. Swann was outraged by their behaviour and inevitably there were arguments and violence. On June 3 he returned home and found the pair together. He told Gallagher to get out. Gallagher refused to go and Emily swore at him. Swann retaliated by throwing a pint pot at her and telling Gallagher he could have her if he wanted her.

The following day Gallagher was heard uttering threats against Swann. He had by now decided to leave Wombwell. On Saturday June 5, he was paid off at the colliery and, on returning to Mrs Ward's, sent out for drink. Soon a drinking session was under way with Gallagher, Emily and Mrs Ward the main participants; also present in the house were Mrs Ward's son and daughter and a man named Wigglesworth. At one point the daughter was sent round to the pawnshop to get Gallagher's jacket and waistcoat out of hock. Late in the afternoon Emily took the garments across to her house and Gallagher followed her. Why she did this is not clear, but when her husband returned at about quarter to six and saw Gallagher coming down the stairs, he was in no doubt what they had been up to. He ordered Gallagher out of the house. Emily protested that he had come to collect some letters and papers which he had left in one of the bedrooms. Swann's response was to beat her.

---

[107] He was regularly seen leaving her house at around 4 a.m.

Minutes later she was across at Mrs Ward's. Drawing back her shawl, she pointed to a black eye. 'See what our Bill has done,' she said. Gallagher was immediately on his feet. 'I will go and give him something for himself,' he said. 'I hope he kills him,' called Emily as she followed after him.

On reaching the Swanns' house, Gallagher forced his way in. There were then sounds of a struggle, above which Emily's voice could be heard shouting encouragement. Five minutes or so later Gallagher was back at Mrs Ward's. 'I have broken four ribs and I will break four more,' he declared. After supping some more ale, he was back across the street. Once again the sounds of a struggle could be heard. A short time afterwards Gallagher returned to Mrs Ward's but Emily did not. He went across for a third time but found the door locked. Emily would later claim that she helped her husband into a chair and gave him some water, but that he slithered off it.

Nearly an hour went by before she emerged from the house. She immediately went to the Wards for help, telling her neighbour that she thought her husband was dead. Mrs Ward, her son and Wigglesworth all went across and found William Swann in the kitchen, lying between a cupboard and a chair; on the floor nearby was a poker. He was obviously dead. Dr Foley was sent for and pronounced life extinct. It was his view that death had taken place about an hour before. It was only now that the police were informed (the police station was a mere 100 yards away from the scene of the killing). They spoke to Emily but could get little sense out of her, which they put down to the drink she had taken.

While Emily was in the house with the door locked, Gallagher, who was still in his working clothes, had got washed. He invited Mrs Ward to go for a drink with him and bought her a whisky in the *Royal Oak*. To the news that Swann was dead, he reacted with glee: laughing, dancing and shouting 'I am not guilty, am I?' Then, with 10s. 6d in his pocket, which he had got by pawning clothes, he caught a train to Sheffield, where he bought a ticket to Bradford. He was now a man on the run and it would be two months before he was arrested.

In the meanwhile the police arranged for a *post-mortem* to be carried out and arrangements were made for the holding of an inquest. The autopsy was performed by a local man, Dr Atkins. He found upwards of 20 bruises on the head and body. In addition four ribs and the breast bone had been broken. The cause of death was bleeding into the brain.

The inquest was opened at 2.45 pm on Tuesday, June 9, in the *Horse Shoe Hotel* by coroner Dossey Wightman. Mr John Robinson, the clerk to the Urban District Council, was foreman of the jury. Emily Swann was the first witness called.[108] She sought to cast the whole of the blame for the death on Gallagher. She insisted that when Gallagher ran across the road, having seen her black eye, she had told him it was nothing to do with him and that he wasn't to go in, but he had done and had started punching and kicking her husband. She tried to pull him off and get her husband up but Gallagher punched her on the chin, knocking her to the floor. When she got up off the floor he was hitting her husband

---

[108] She appeared with her left eye heavily bandaged.

with an arm chair. He then called her husband a bastard and left the house. She lifted her husband into a chair and tried to give him some water but he slithered down onto the floor. She then went across to Mrs Ward and told her that she thought Gallagher had very nearly killed her husband but she (Mrs Ward) would have nothing to do with the matter. Cross-examined, she said she could not send for the doctor until she had got someone into the house.

Walter Wigglesworth, however, told a different story. He said that when Gallagher went across to the Swanns, Emily followed after saying 'I hope he punches him to death.'

After a short summing up by the coroner and a brief consultation among themselves the jury returned a verdict of 'wilful murder against John Gallagher,' adding that that the testimony against Mrs Swann posed the question whether she was not guilty in some shape or form. The coroner thereupon issued a warrant for Gallagher's arrest. After the inquest Emily remained behind in the public house in the hope that the large crowd, which had gathered outside, would disperse. It did not and when she eventually left she was 'hooted' and had to be protected by the police.

The funeral was the next day. Fearing that her presence among the mourners would lead to disorder the police advised Emily to stay away, which she did. The coffin was preceded by workmen from Aldham bottle works, where the deceased had been employed, with the coffin bearers chosen from amongst their number.

On August 4, Gallagher was arrested at his sister's home in Middlesbrough. The police at Barnsley were immediately informed by telegraph, and that same day they arrested Emily and charged her with murder. The next morning the couple appeared before the Barnsley West Riding magistrates and were remanded in custody to Wakefield prison. Their committal hearing took place 12 days later on August 18. By now the police had traced a number of further witnesses. Of these by far the most damaging to the accused was John William Dunn, a miner, who lived at 45, George Square, and who from his kitchen could see into the Swanns' house. He described how at about 6 o' clock on the day in question he saw Gallagher standing at the Swanns' door. The door was closed but Gallagher shook it so violently that it flew open. He then went inside and shouted 'I will coffin the____ before morning.' The door then closed and a scuffle took place inside during which he (Dunn) heard Mrs Swann shout 'Give it to him, Johnny' many times. That went on for about ten minutes. Then Gallagher came out, went into Mrs Ward's and took a drink from a pot on the table. He then went back to the Swanns, saying as he got to the door 'I will murder the swine before morning. If he can't kick a man, he shan't kick a woman.' There was then the same sort of scuffling as before, with Mrs Swann shouting encouragement as before. When Gallagher next came out he had blood on his face and Mrs Swann was holding his hand.[109]

---

[109] A witness named Beard said he had heard Swann come up to Gallagher and say 'You've done it' or 'We've done it.'

Neither accused was represented and neither gave evidence nor called any witnesses. At the conclusion of the evidence both were committed for trial at the next Leeds Assizes.

They were tried on December 9, 1903 at Leeds Town Hall before Mr Justice Darling. Mr Tindal Atkinson KC and Mr W J Waugh prosecuted on behalf of the Treasury; Gallagher was defended, at the request of the judge, by Mr Mitchell Innes and Swann by Mr Harold Newell. The Crown evidence followed the same course as at the inquest and the committal hearing. Neither accused gave evidence nor called any witnesses.[110] Mr Mitchell Innes, for Gallagher, submitted that it was not until Mrs Swann showed him her bruises that his client showed any malice against Swann; he acted under the influence of drink and provocation and a struggle ensued. The verdict should be one of manslaughter. For the prisoner Swann, Mr Newell appealed to the jury not to convict on intemperate words. Her actions showed that she did not wish her husband done to death, but rather that he should have nothing more than a good thumping for what he had done. The judge in summing up commented on the ability of the defence and paid a particular tribute to the speech of Mr Mitchell Innes. As to the relative guilt of the two prisoners, he directed the jury that one did not commit murder only with one's own hand. If one person instigated another to commit murder, and that other did, the instigator was also guilty of murder. After forty minutes' deliberation the jury found both accused guilty of murder. Asked if she had anything to say why sentence of death should not be

---

[110] Emily had, it seems, been contemplating giving evidence and calling her 11-year-old-daughter as a witness, but was persuaded against doing so.

passed, Emily replied 'Yes, I am innocent. I am not afraid of immediate death because I am innocent and will go to God.' The judge, having observed that there could be no doubt that the verdict was the right one, proceeded to pass sentence of death. As he did so both accused appeared unmoved. As she left the dock Emily, smiled and waved to a friend in the public gallery.

After verdict it was revealed that the prosecution had kept back from the jury a statement made by Gallagher in which he had claimed that Swann had killed the deceased with a poker, after he had punched and kicked him.[111] In the opinion of Dr Atkins the fatal head injury could have been caused either by kicks or by blows with the poker found near the body.

Following their conviction both accused were lodged in Armley gaol to await execution.[112] During their time in the condemned cell both displayed penitence. Gallagher from the beginning entertained little hope of a reprieve. Not so Emily Swann: she was convinced that the fact that she had young children would weigh heavily in her favour.

On Christmas Day the couple saw each other, for the first time since the trial, at a special service in the prison chapel, after which they were taken back to their cells to eat Christmas dinner.

On Monday 28th they were informed by the prison governor that there would be no reprieve and that they would hang at

---

[111] If she did, it was not the first time she used a weapon. The witness Dunn, at the committal hearing, said he had seen her attack Swann with a hammer in May, a month before the killing (*Sheffield Telegraph*, August 19, 1903).

[112] At this time those convicted of murder had no right of appeal against conviction but could petition for mercy. Petitions for mercy were sent on Emily's behalf first to the Home Office and, when this failed, to the King.

9 o'clock the next morning.[113] When hangmen Billington and Ellis arrived outside Gallagher's cell a little before 9 a.m. they found him resigned and unresisting. He was pinioned and then led a short distance from the cell to a position where he would be out of sight of Swann when she emerged from her cell. When the executioners went to her cell they found her prostrate and hysterical. They advised the wardresses to give her brandy. This, according to Ellis, 'put new life into her. In a couple of minutes she was more or less normal. We were now able to pinion her arms behind her back. Something which would have been out of the question a few moments previously.' The procession now set off for the scaffold led by the chaplain, followed by Gallagher with two warders at his side and then Emily with a wardress at each side. By the time Emily reached the scaffold Gallagher was already on the trap with the white cap over his head. As the rope was being placed around his neck, she suddenly cried out 'Good Morning, John.' Gallagher, who had no idea that she was there, started violently then replied 'Good morning, love.' As the rope was being placed around her neck Emily again spoke. 'Good-bye and God bless you.' The lever was then pulled.

After an inquest within the prison, at which the jury was told that death was instantaneous in both cases, the bodies were buried within the prison.

---

[113] After receiving the news, Emily dictated heart-rending letters to her 80-year-old mother and her sisters, begging them to love her daughters Eleanor and 'Little Ellie,' and to give little Raymond a kiss from her.

A large crowd, including many women and girls, assembled outside the prison gates before the execution and, despite the coldness of the morning, a small number stayed until the inquest jury departed.

Ethel Major

Until the late eighteenth century, Hull had its own assizes and gallows.[114] In 1794, however, the town gave up its assizes, the work being transferred to York, which now became the place of execution for Hull criminals. This remained the position until July,1900 when, following the closure of York Castle Prison, the Hedon Road Gaol[115] in Hull was made a hanging prison. Between 1902 and 1934 ten prisoners were put to death there, of whom the last was Ethel Lillie Major. Not only was she the only woman to be hanged in the city in modern times, she was also the last woman to be executed in Yorkshire.

Ethel Major came not from Yorkshire but Lincolnshire and, indeed, was tried and sentenced to death at Lincoln.

When she was 23 she had an illegitimate child.[116] In order to avoid scandal, her parents took in the little girl and passed her off as their child. Not long after giving birth, Ethel bumped into Arthur Major whom she had not seen since school. They started

---

[114] The gallows were at Myton Carr just outside the city walls where Great Thornton Street is today. The last execution there was that of John Rogerson in 1778 for coining. The gallows themselves were not actually removed until 1811 (*Victoria History of England, Kingston upon Hull*, p 210 and Angus Young, *More Murders of Hull*, Highgate of Beverley, 1996, p. 10).
[115] The jail, which is two miles out of the city centre, was opened in 1870 as a prison for both sexes.
[116] Iris Tryphen.

walking out together and in the summer of 1918 they were married. In May 1920 Ethel gave birth to a son, Lawrence Arthur. In 1929 the family moved to a bungalow on the outskirts of Horncastle. At around this time, Ethel either confessed or let slip to her husband the fact that she had had an illegitimate child, and that the girl, whom he thought was her younger sister, was in fact her daughter. He took the news badly and the marriage was soon in trouble. He began drinking and when in drink he would beat her and their son. He also started womanising. To protect her son from his violence she had her parents take him in. On several occasions she left home herself but always ended up going back.[117]

In the Spring of 1934 things took a decided turn for the worse when Ethel found amongst her husband's belongings two love letters signed Rose. Convinced that they had been written by Rose Kettleborough, she told all who would listen that her husband was having an affair with Mrs Kettleborough.[118] On May 1, 1934 she showed the letters to her doctor. 'Now you can understand why I've been ill,' she told him. 'A man like that is not fit to live, I will do him.'

Before the month's end Arthur Major was dead. On May 22 he became ill after eating a meal of corned beef and died two days

---

[117] One of the accusations which Arthur always made against her was that she was extravagant and on the 20th May, 1934 (only four days before his death) the *Horncastle News* received for publication a notice from him stating that he would not be responsible for her debts, and that she had no authority to make any statements or give any notice on his behalf.

[118] Those she informed about the letters included her father, her doctor, Rose Kettleborough's husband, a solicitor and an official of the local authority. There is little doubt that Mrs Kettleborough had, despite her denials, written the letters; in one of them the name Major was spelt Majar and, as the judge at Ethel's trial pointed out to the jury, the same spelling mistake was to be found in another letter which Mrs Kettleborough admitted having written.

later. The doctor who attended him, after being told by Ethel that her husband had had one of his fits, certified death as due to *status epilepticus.*[119]

The day after Arthur Major died the police received an anonymous letter. Signed 'Fairplay,' it read:

'Have you heard of a wife poisoning her husband? Look further into the death of Mr Major of Kirkby-on-Bain. Why did he complain of his food tasting nasty and throw it away to a neighbour's dog, which has since died? Ask the undertaker if he looked natural after death. Why did he stiffen so quickly? Why was he so jerky when dying? I myself have heard her threaten to poison him years ago. I beg you to analyse the contents of his stomach.'

The police had no option but to follow up the letter and, when they did, they discovered that what it said about the dog appeared to be true. 'I saw Ethel Major feed something off a plate to Mr Maltby's dog the night before Arthur Major died' neighbour Ethel Roberts told police officers. 'She smiled as the dog ate the scraps and laughed out loud as she went back into her house.'[120] The dog, which had died not long after, was buried in the Maltbys' garden. The police had it dug up and its stomach contents examined. They contained strychnine. The coroner was immediately informed.

---

[119] A condition in which there is a rapid succession of epileptic fits.
[120] The Maltbys were the Majors' next-door neighbours. According to Mrs Roberts, Mrs Major normally discouraged dogs and on one occasion had thrown a bath at a dog which came to her back door.

On Sunday May 27, the day set for the funeral,[121] Ethel Major received a visit from Police Sergeant Mitchell, who told her that the coroner had ordered a *post-mortem* and that the funeral would have to be postponed. 'I'm not under suspicion, am I?' she asked. 'I've done nothing wrong.' The officer was non-committal.

The *post-mortem* on Arthur Major established that he too had died of strychnine poisoning.

The police had, by now, discovered that Ethel's father Tom Brown, a retired gamekeeper, had a box in which he kept strychnine and other poisons which he used to kill vermin. At their request he produced the box which was locked. He confirmed that Ethel knew about the strychnine but claimed that she would not have been able to get into the box because the key had been lost ten years before and never replaced.

When questioned by Chief Inspector Young from Scotland Yard Ethel said 'I didn't know where he kept his poisons. I never at any time had any poison in the house,' adding 'I didn't know my husband died of strychnine.' 'I never mentioned strychnine,' the inspector interrupted. 'How did you know about that?' 'Oh, I'm sorry,' she replied, 'I must have made a mistake.' This was the second unfortunate remark she had made since the police first came to see her but worse was to come. When the house was searched, in the larger of the two back bedrooms a suitcase was found. In it was clothing and a purse. In the purse was a key to the

---

[121] The deceased's brother had protested that Sunday was too early for the funeral, but Ethel said that the rector was going away on Monday and she would like him to conduct the service; also her son Lawrence had the chance of some work on the Monday.

poison box and its shiny condition indicated that it had been used recently[122].

Ethel Major stood trial for murder at Lincoln Assizes on October 29, 1934 before Mr Justice Charles.[123] She was represented by Norman Birkett KC, an advocate with a deservedly high reputation as a criminal defender. Birkett called no evidence[124] but, in a powerful closing speech, argued that the Crown had not proved their case beyond reasonable doubt. If the accused really were guilty, he contended, she would have thrown the key of the box away. Nor would she have given some of the poisoned corn beef to the neighbour's dog. After an hour's retirement the jury were back in court with a guilty verdict and a strong recommendation to mercy.[125]

Notice of appeal was lodged on the grounds that the summing up was unfair.[126] The Court of Criminal Appeal would have none of it. The summing up, declared Lord Chief Justice Hewart, was perfectly fair and sufficient.

---

[122] 'It was quite polished and had the appearance of being carried about,' was how the Chief Inspector put it.
[123] The trial lasted four days. Mr Richard O'Sullivan KC and Mr P E Sandlands appeared for the Crown.
[124] The accused's failure to give evidence was commented upon by the judge who told the jury 'You may think it a misfortune that we have not heard the evidence she might have given on oath before you.' (*Hull Daily Mail*, November 1, 1934)
[125] For long periods during [the] final day of the trial Mrs Major sat silently weeping with her head wearily resting on the shoulders of a wardress. During the summing up [she] fainted. She had been sitting quietly in the dock when suddenly her head and body slumped forward. A wardress prevented her falling to the floor....She seemed to have aged ten years waiting for the verdict. [After sentence] she was carried from the court on the shoulders of a warder with a wardress holding each of her hands. Her wails from the cells below could plainly be heard in the court corridors and men and women wept freely.' (*Hull Daily Mail*, November 1, 1934)
[126] Whilst conceding that, speaking generally, the summing up was not only fair and accurate but on many vital matters favourable to the accused, Birkett argued that the jury should have been directed that one possible inference to be drawn from the evidence was that the deceased had committed suicide (*Hull Daily Mail*, December 3, 1934).

A petition for a reprieve was lodged but, on December 16, the Home Secretary announced that there would be no reprieve. Ethel Major would be executed in three days' time. The news came as a profound shock both to the condemned woman and to the city of Hull. No woman had been executed in Britain since Louie Calvert in 1926 and it had been assumed that the jury's recommendation to mercy would be enough to save Ethel Major. However, those familiar with the ways of the Home Office knew that recommendations to mercy often went unheeded and that poisoners were rarely spared.

With time fast running out, Alderman Stark, the Lord Mayor of Hull, despatched a telegram to the Home Secretary asking for mercy for the condemned woman.

> *The impending execution is most distressing to 1000s of women who reside near the prison...The citizens of Hull would have taken active measures some time ago in an appeal for clemency had it not been for the jury's strong recommendation to mercy, which we thought all along would have led to a reprieve.*

Copies of the telegram were sent the Prime Minister, to George Lansbury and the four Members of Parliament for Hull. Similar telegrams were also dispatched by President of Hull City Labour Party. The Hull Socialist League appealed to Sir Stafford Cripps to intervene. But the Home Secretary would not budge. In the early hours of December 18, the Mayor redoubled his efforts sending off further telegrams to the King, the Queen and the Home Office. They fell on stony ground.

After learning that there would be no reprieve, Ethel Major became hysterical and her screams could be heard all over the prison.[127] It is said that the governor, in an attempt to bring her some solace, arranged for a local orchestra to come and play for her.[128] On the day before her execution she was in a state of total collapse with the doctor constantly in attendance. Her last visitor was her 15-year-old son, Lawrence, who had been a witness at her trial. Her last half hour on earth she spent with the chaplain. She was hanged at 9 a.m. by Thomas Pierrepoint. Outside the prison gates about 300 people, mainly men, had gathered.

It is clear that the Mayor's description of the impact of the execution upon those living nearby was no exaggeration. One woman in the crowd said 'We who live near the prison have spent an anxious night. Here we are in the middle of Christmas preparations with streamers and presents and expectations; all of us could not sleep for thinking of her and what she was bound to be going through.'

In her book *On the Gallows*, Mrs Violet van der Elst, who in the 1930s was a prominent and vociferous campaigner against capital punishment, asserted that

> *If [Mrs Major] had been reprieved, in three months she would have gone to a higher Judge as she had cancer of the throat and could not have lived longer than that*

---

[127] On December 17 she wrote despairingly to her father 'Cannot something be done to save me?' (*Yorkshire Evening Post*, December 17 1934).
[128] Another version has it that the proposal was that the Women's Institute should come and sing carols for her.

If that was truly the case, it is surprising that more was not made of the fact by those campaigning for a reprieve.[129]

If the case shows anything it is how little notice officialdom took of recommendations to mercy in the 1930s.

---

[129] An even more astonishing claim made by Mrs van der Elst is that the hanging resulted in Ethel being decapitated. Nothing was said at the post-execution inquest to indicate that anything untoward had occurred and it is difficult believe that Mrs van der Elst is right about this. She is certainly wrong when she says that Ethel's trial was at the Old Bailey

PART 2

JUDGES BEHAVING BADLY

Sir Jonah Barrington

After the 'Glorious Revolution' of 1688, in an attempt to secure the independence of the judges, their terms of appointment were altered: henceforth they would hold office not, as formerly, during the king's pleasure, but during good behaviour.[130] In 1700 the change was made law, the Act of Settlement providing that judges should hold office during good behaviour but be removable by the Crown upon an address of both Houses of Parliament. This is still the law today although the protection given extends only to judges of the superior courts (that is the High Court and above), circuit judges, district judges and other lesser judicial office holders being simply removable by the Lord Chancellor for either incapacity or misconduct.

Only one judge has ever been removed under the procedure laid down in the Act of Settlement: Sir Jonah Barrington.

Born in 1760 of 'a good protestant family of the Pale,'[131] Jonah Barrington was the fourth child of John Barrington, a landowner in Queen's County. Educated at Trinity College, Dublin, he had originally been destined for the army and actually received the offer of an ensign's commission from General Hunt Walsh. However, upon learning that his intended regiment was likely to be ordered into immediate service in America, he wrote

---

[130] For the evils of the former system, see F W Maitland, *The Constitutional History of England*, Cambridge University Press, 1968, p. 312 'Throughout the Stuart reigns, judges have been dismissed if they withstand the king – too often they have been his servile creatures. All along they have held their offices *durante beneplacito* – during the king's good pleasure.'

[131] The Pale – a name formerly given to that part of Ireland, in Dublin, Kildare, Meath and Louth, which was completely under English rule in distinction to the parts where the old Irish laws and customs prevailed.

declining the offer and asking that the favour 'be [bestowed] upon some hardier soldier.'

The career he eventually settled on was the law. Called to the bar in 1788, he made great strides in his new profession, taking silk only five years later. Some sourly attributed his rapid rise to 'his position and his social qualifications … [rather than his] legal knowledge.'

By the time he was made a KC he was already a member of the Irish parliament. He was elected MP for Tuam in 1790 for which he sat until 1797. Having declined to repurchase the Tuam seat, he was then out of politics until 1798 when he was elected for Clogher. In the same year he was appointed judge of the Irish Court of Admiralty, an office carrying a salary of £500 per annum (later increased to £1,000). In 1799 he was offered but refused the office of solicitor- general. At the election of 1802 he unsuccessfully contested Dublin. This marked the end of his political career.

Extravagant by nature, he was, by the time he was knighted in 1807, heavily in debt. In later life, he humorously described some of the more harmless shifts to which he was reduced to extricate himself from his difficulties. What he did not, however, trouble to tell his readers was that in 1805 he had gone so far as to 'borrow' some of the money which had been paid into his court to abide the outcome of lawsuits, an offence which he repeated on at least two further occasions (in 1806 and 1810). Pineau, the registrar of the court, sought to conceal the judge's defalcations by making good part of the deficiency out of his own pocket, believing that Barrington would in due course reimburse him. He did not and, in 1810, a salvor who had a claim to part of the missing monies petitioned the court for payment. Barrington sent him a cheque for £40 under his own hand which he asked him not to present for two months. In about 1819 he decamped to France, appointing deputies to discharge the duties of his office.[132] It is alleged that on the eve of his departure he took the opportunity to perpetrate an audacious fraud

> *He had pledged his family plate for a considerable sum to Mr John Stevenson, pawnbroker, and member of the Common Council. 'My dear fellow,' said the knight, condescendingly, as he dropped in one day to that person's prinite closet, ' I am in a d---l of a hobble. I asked, quite impromptu, the Lord-Lieutenant, Chancellor, and Judges, to dine with me, forgetting how awkwardly I was situated; and, by Jove, they have written to say they'll come! Of course I could not entertain them without the plate; I shall require it for that evening only; but it must be on due condition - that you come yourself to the dinner and represent the Corporation. Bring the plate with you, and take it back again, at night.' The pawnbroker was dazzled; although not usually given to nepotism, he obligingly embraced the proposal. During dinner, and after it, Sir Jonah plied his 'uncle' well with wine. The pawnbroker had a bad head for potation, though a good one for valuation; he fell asleep and under the table almost simultaneously; and when he awoke to full consciousness, Sir Jonah, accompanied by the plate, had nearly reached Boulogne, never again to visit his native land!*[133]

Nor, apparently, was this his only 'haul'

---

[132] See *The Dublin Patriot*, December 29, 1822 and *Carrick's Morning Post*, January 1, 1823 which describe him as having lived in Boulogne for the last three years, his duties having been discharged in his absence by three very competent gentlemen, Mr Aspinall, Mr Mahaffy and Mr Holwell Walshe.'

[133] K Finlay, *Sir Jonah Barrington*, webpage http//indigo.ie/~kfinlay/shamsquire/barrington.htm).

> *Mr Fennell Collins, a rich saddler, who resided in Dame Street, [was induced to lend] 'the Judge' £3,000, on what seemed tolerable security; [not] one farthing of the money [did he ever see again].* 134

For the next 15 years or thereabouts, Barrington lived in France continuing to draw his judicial salary and discharging the duties of his office through deputies. Periodically he received letters from Pineau requesting repayment which produced equivocating and evasive answers but no money. By now he must have believed that he would never be called to account. However, in 1828 he received a nasty shock. Parliament that year appointed commissioners to report on the Irish Courts and, in the course of their inquiries into the jurisdiction and organisation of the Admiralty court, his defalcations came to light. The commissioners invited him to attend before them in Dublin. He declined pleading ill health. Letters requesting his explanations of and comments upon what they had found elicited merely a denial of any wrongdoing. Eventually they ran out of patience. Their report which confined itself to a statement of what they had found was damning.

> '*[In December 1805] the ship Nancy and its cargo ... were sold by the marshal under a commission of appraisement ... in this cause alone Sir Jonah Barrington appropriated to his own use out of the proceeds £482, 8s. 8d. and £200, making together £682, 8s. 8d., and never repaid any part of either; and ... the registrar is a loser in that cause to the amount of £546, 11s. 4d. ...[On the 12th January 1810, the sum of £200 was paid into court on account of the proceeds in the cause of The Redstrand],*

---

[134] Ibid.

and the same day Sir Jonah Barrington, by an order in his own handwriting which has been produced to us, directed the registrar to lodge that sum to his (the judge's) credit in the bank of Sir William Gleadowe Newcomen, which he accordingly did.'[135]

Upon receiving the report the Commons appointed a select committee to investigate the allegations against the judge. After taking evidence and giving Sir Jonah the opportunity to offer his answer to the charges against him, the committee declared itself satisfied that he had indeed been guilty of misappropriation.

In May, 1830 the Commons met to consider what action to take on the select committee report. Before the debate got under way counsel for Barrington was permitted to address the House on behalf of his client. The procedure which had been adopted was, he argued, unjust. Allegations of criminal misappropriation were for a jury to pronounce upon not a committee of the House. A couple of members spoke up for Barrington, one suggesting that he ought to be given the opportunity to cross-examine and call witnesses and another contending that, since the registrar of the Admiralty court was its banker and as such entitled to lend court funds to whomsoever he chose, all that Sir Jonah appeared to have done was to borrow money from one who had authority to lend it (a remark which drew from another member the tart retort that '[if he] had borrowed money he had borrowed it as gentlemen borrow money on Hounslow Heath.'[136]) But most members thought that the matter had gone on long enough. The evidence against the judge was overwhelming, he had been given every

---

[135] Eighteenth Report on Courts of Justice in Ireland, PP 1829 (293.) IV, 1, pp 9-10.
[136] A reference to highwaymen.

opportunity to make his answer to the charges but had failed to do so. An address for his removal should be drawn up without further delay.

On June 14 the matter came before the Lords. They decided to adopt a more formal procedure than had the Commons. The case against the judge was outlined by the Attorney-General, who then proceeded to call evidence. His principal witness was Pineau. His testimony and the documentation he produced was damning. On July 17 Barrington's counsel opened his defence. His client was, he contended, a man of unimpeachable integrity. The real delinquent was Pineau as he would now proceed to prove. The witnesses he called in fact proved nothing of the sort and, on July 20, the House resolved to join with the Commons in the address for removal.

But Barrington still had a final card to play. Many years before he had received a letter from William IV, then Duke of Clarence, thanking him for a kindness he had shown to his mistress on a visit to Dublin and expressing the hope that it might at some future time be in his power to attest his appreciation of kindness so disinterested and, following his dismissal, he sent the letter to the King. It is said that he received two letters by return post, the first a rather stiff reply saying that no one knew better than Sir Jonah Barrington the very material difference which existed between the Duke of Clarence and the King of England, and that it was impossible to recognise, in his then position, every acquaintance whom he might have known when acting in a comparatively subordinate capacity, the second a private letter granting him a pension out of the privy purse equal to his forfeited judicial salary. [137]

Sir Jonah, who never returned to Ireland, died at Versailles on April 8 1834. He spent his last years writing works on Irish history, the best known being *Rise and Fall of the Irish Nation* (1833)[138] and *Personal Sketches of his Own Times*, (1827-32).[139]

Although Barrington was the only judge ever to be removed for the misappropriating court funds, the way in which such funds were handled had long been a scandal.

> *[In the eighteenth century the funds in chancery were] under the absolute control of the Chancery Master[s] who [were] not bound to account for any interest received. As the money in court was constantly increasing, the interest formed a handsome addition to the Masters' income. But they were not content with this. They tried to increase their incomes still further by speculation.*
>
> *Shortly after the bursting of the South Sea Bubble (1725) rumours were heard that all was not right with the money in court. An enquiry was ordered [in] consequence of which the Lord Chancellor, Lord Mansfield was impeached and a deficit, which was finally found to amount to £100,871. 6s .8d, was discovered in the accounts of four of the Masters. In consequence, two Acts were passed which deprived the Masters of control of the suitors' money, and placed it in the Bank of England under the control of a new official called the Accountant-General of the Court of Chancery,*[140]

---

[137] K Finlay, op.cit.

[138] Described by George Birmingham in the introduction to *Recollections of Sir Jonah Barrington*, Dublin, 1918 as 'probably as interesting and certainly as untrustworthy as any history book ever written.'

[139] The general verdict on the anecdotes is amusing but unreliable, Sir Jonah not being a man to allow the truth to get in the way of a good story. It was said of him by one commentator that he '[had] as much notion of blushing as a blind man has of colours.'

[140] Sir Wm Holdsworth, *A History of English Law*, Sweet & Maxwell, London (1971 reprint), i, p 440; as late as the 1820s the Registrar of the English Court of Admiralty was permitted to keep for himself the interest on monies in court in Prize Cases; at the beginning of the nineteenth century it was discovered that a considerable quantity of Chancery records had been stolen, presumably by officials, and sold for waste paper (Holdsworth ibid.)

Thirty one years after Barrington's death, it came to light that Wilde, the Leeds bankruptcy registrar, had been allowed to retire on pension, despite clear evidence that he had been guilty of misappropriation of court funds.[141] A select committee enquiry revealed an alarming state of affairs

> *' [On Wilde's resignation his] office was given to a barrister named Walsh, who had lent large sums of money to ... [Lord] Chancellor [Westbury's] son Richard, who had represented that he could influence the disposal of the Chancellor's patronage. Richard's extravagance was notorious; he had recently been compelled to resign as an undischarged bankrupt. Westbury had refused to give his son another appointment but it was rumoured that Walsh was only holding the Leeds registrarship until Westbury could appoint his son to it. The ...Select Committee reported that Wilde should not have been granted a pension and that Walsh's appointment showed corruption on part of Westbury's officials.'[142]*

So far as Parliament was concerned, all this was very much a case of *déjà vu*. In February 1865, Westbury had been instrumental in securing the grant of a pension to Edmunds, a clerk in the House of Lords and clerk to the Commissioners of Patents who had resigned both offices, but had not seen fit to disclose to the House that proposed to appoint his son to the office in the Lords which Edmunds had vacated, nor that the true reason for the latter's resignation was that he had converted some £18,000 of public money to his own use.[143] Having been censured

---

[141] Between 1852 and 1864 he had failed to pay monies received by him as Clerk into the Treasury but had, instead, placed them in a bank account in his own name and had kept the interest earned for himself. He had also been of other defalcations and of neglect of duty.

[142] Holdsworth, op. cit., xvi, 80.

[143] Edmunds' defalcations were first exposed in early 1864; the scandal surrounding his resignation of his Lords' clerkship was the subject of a Select Committee inquiry, which reported in May 1865 (see *The Times*, May 5, 1865); *Punch's* verdict on the Report was that 'it amounts to this: that the conduct of Mr Edmunds in using public money has been too bad and that of the Lord Chancellor in not exposing him has been too good.' (*The Times*, May 11, 1865).

by the House of Commons for his inattention to the public interest, Westbury resigned.[144]

The Shropshire Coroner

In 1823 occurred one of the worst cases of judicial corruption in the last 200 years. It excited only local interest at the time and has long since been forgotten.[145]

Edmund Whitecombe, a surgeon with a substantial midwifery practice, had been elected one of the four county coroners for Shropshire in 1818. As such it was his duty to conduct inquests into all sudden and suspicious deaths which occurred in his part of the county. If the inquest jury returned a verdict of murder or manslaughter by a named person, it was his duty as coroner to commit that person to the Assizes for trial. Just such a death occurred on the night of January 23-24, 1823. At a little after 8 pm a servant at Severn Hall, in the parish of Astley Abbots, had found 40-year-old Sarah Newton collapsed on the floor, bleeding heavily from her private parts. A surgeon was sent for but to no avail: by 1 a.m. she was dead. Sarah was the wife of John Newton, a well-to-do farmer and the tenant of the Hall. She had married him ten years before, had had four children by him and was expecting a fifth. Her death was notified to Whitecombe who announced that he would hold an inquest at the Hall the

---

[144] Ibid. xvi, 79-80.
[145] The account which follows is based upon the reports of the trials of the two principals published in the *Salopian Journal*, 12 February, 21 March, 7 May, July 30 and August 6 1823 and *The Times*, 24 March, 31 March, 2 June, 1 August and 14 November, 1823; see also (1823) 1 C & P 124.

following Monday, and gave instructions for a jury panel be summoned.

Monday the 27th dawned cold and wet. During the morning jurors arrived in dribs and drabs followed at 11 a.m. by the coroner himself. Like the jurors, Whitecombe was doubtless anxious to get the whole dismal business over quickly and there seemed a good chance that he would be able to do so. There was talk of a miscarriage and, if that were true, the case would not detain the jury long. In fact, it would prove anything but straightforward. The dead woman had marks to her face which strongly suggested that she had been beaten. Two of the servants went out of their way to make sure the coroner knew about these injuries and, after speaking to them, he went upstairs to the bedroom where the body lay. When he returned he gave instructions for a message to be taken to James Coley, a Bridgnorth surgeon, asking him to attend to carry out an autopsy.

By the time Coley arrived the jury panel was becoming restive. It was 3 p.m. and still the inquest had not got under way. Coley immediately busied himself in making an external examination of the body. He was struck by the number of injuries the dead woman had: a black eye, a cut lip, a cut to her chest, a bruised and dislocated finger, bruising to one of her armpits and to both shins. He remarked that one of the marks on her shin looked to have been caused by a kick. 'Oh no,' said Whitecombe, 'she has burnt her shins at the fire.' As soon as the body was opened up it became clear what the source of the haemorrhage was. Several internal blood vessels had ruptured. Coley was in no doubt that the ruptures had been caused by a violent kick or punch.

Events now took an astonishing turn. Once the body had been sewn up the coroner went to speak to the waiting jury panel. The case was not, he told them, as serious as had been thought; there was no question of a criminal charge against anyone and he proposed to release half of them and proceed with just twelve jurors. Coley protested. There was plain evidence of homicide and yet the jurors were being told that crime was ruled out. The coroner ignored him. Once the unwanted jurors had left, he told the twelve who remained that they were required by law to view the body, but added that they need do no more than satisfy themselves that the deceased was lying dead in the bedroom upstairs. Taking him at his word, the jurors looked into the room where she lay covered in a sheet with only her head visible, and walked out again. One later said that he doubted if the jury spent more than half a minute in the room. Once they had reassembled downstairs, they were sworn and the inquest got under way.

Over the next five hours the jury heard evidence from farm servants, from Coley and from Barber the surgeon who had attended the deceased on the night she died. One witness spoke of a quarrel between the deceased and her husband on the night of her death but the matter was not gone into. There was also mention of Edwards, a Bridgnorth tinsmith, having visited the Hall just before 8 p.m. that night but he was not sent for. If the deposition which the coroner took of Barber's evidence can be trusted (and Barber would later disown it), he was prevailed upon to say that he could not tell how the fatal bleeding had been caused. Coley was of sterner stuff and made it clear that in his opinion it had been caused by violence. Might there not asked the coroner be some other explanation? Suppose she had fallen over a stile might that explain her internal injuries? 'I think that highly improbable,' replied Coley. The coroner tried another tack. 'Might not the bleeding have been caused by the heavy work, baking and brewing, which the deceased had been doing earlier in the day?' 'No,' said Coley. The surgeon started to tell the jury about the facial injuries. He was at once cut short. Had they anything to do with the death? No, then the jury could ignore them. Once the evidence was concluded the coroner summed up with great partiality pressing the jury to the view that death was due to natural causes. They retired but were soon back with a question: how had the bleeding been caused? The coroner dismissed them angrily. 'What, would you hang the man?' he exclaimed. Eventually they returned with a verdict 'Died by bleeding, but how caused is to us unknown.' 'That' said the coroner ' is died by visitation of God'. 'No,' said the jury, ' that is not what we mean.' At the insistence of a local magistrate, the verdict was recorded as returned but with the gloss that 'the deceased, who was six months pregnant, had on the day of the fatal haemorrhage been hard at work brewing and baking.'

The verdict caused great dissatisfaction in the locality: the talk was that if the jury has heard what Edwards, the tinsmith, had to say, John Newton would have been committed for trial for murder. Edwards had called at the Hall at around 7 pm on the

Wednesday night with his bill. Newton, on checking it, saw that one of the items he was being charged for was a lantern his wife had been given money to pay for. In a temper he shouted for her accusing her of keeping the money for herself. Edwards tried to calm him down: rather than see the matter a source of discord between them, he would forget the lantern. Newton would not hear of it and paid him in full. Edwards then made to leave and called out 'Good night Mrs Newton'. He got no reply. 'She's hiding, she knows what to expect,' said Newton. Again Edwards sought to intercede, telling Newton that if he hit his wife he would never speak to him again.

Edwards' account tied in with what the servants had to say. Shortly after his departure, a girl returning to the Hall across the fields had heard one of the Newton children shout 'Please dad don't,' and, on entering the building, had found the deceased lying on the floor bleeding. Other servants told how, after they had got her to bed, Newton had continued to berate her about the bill, asking her who was the greater villain she or he. The coroner's jury had been misled. There was no mystery about Sarah Newton's death. Her husband, a practised wife-beater, had simply given her one beating too many.

Within days of the inquest the coroner received a visit from an attorney instructed by her family. The neighbourhood was dissatisfied with the verdict and the jury wished to change it if they could. The coroner sympathised. He had no doubt in his own mind that Newton had killed his wife, but there was no evidence to prove it. He was sorry but there was nothing he could do.

The family were not willing to be fobbed off. They went next to the local magistrates who acted with commendable despatch. Newton was arrested and brought before them for preliminary examination on a charge of murder and, after hearing evidence from Edwards, the farm servants and no less than three surgeons, they committed him to the Shrewsbury Spring Assizes to stand trial.

The case came on before Mr Justice Best on Saturday, March 22, 1823. In a statement from the dock Newton claimed that his wife had attacked him when he was in liquor. 'She struck me first. What I did was in a passion and I did not think any harm.' His counsel suggested he had been insane at the time of the killing and called witnesses who spoke of there being a history of madness in the family, and said that Newton had long been considered insane by those who knew him. None of this cut any ice with the jury who, after a retirement of just three minutes, brought in a verdict of guilty. Sentence of death was passed with the execution set for the following Monday.

On the 24th Newton was hanged in front of a huge crowd. He had told a gentleman, who had visited him after the verdict, that on the fatal night he had struck and kicked his wife several times and would have killed the child who tried to stop him, had the boy not managed to escape from him. On his walk to the scaffold he was heard to remark that he had lost the best wife in the world for three shillings.

The magistrates now turned their fire on the coroner. In May 1823 they were granted leave by the Court of King's Bench to prefer an information against him for corruption.

The case came on for trial on July 29 at the Shrewsbury Summer Assizes before Mr Baron Hullock and a special jury.[146] The court room was packed as Mr Pearson, counsel for the Crown, got to his feet. The accusation against the coroner was that he had rigged the inquest into Sarah Newton's death in the hope of receiving a bribe for his trouble from the husband. Edwards, the tinsmith, servants from the Hall, three surgeons, the foreman and two members of the jury panel were called by the Crown.

Counsel for Whitecombe in his opening argued strongly for an acquittal. His client had never met Newton before the day of the inquest, and the only conversation he had with him that day had been to ask him to provide stabling and fodder for his horses. Undoubtedly, the coroner had been mistaken when he had attributed the bleeding to a natural cause, but he had been misled by remarks made by the farm servants 'which had left an impression on his mind which he could not banish.' Did not the fact that he had insisted that an experienced surgeon be sent for to perform the autopsy testify to the purity of his intentions? He then proceeded to call a large number of witnesses, including no less than nine witnesses as to character.

It was late in the evening when the judge began his summing up. The coroner had, he told the jury, been guilty of a

---

[146] A jury composed of men who were bankers, merchants or of the rank of esquire of above.

gross dereliction of duty in causing the body to be dissected before it was inspected by the jurors and in subsequently telling them that a close examination was not requisite. It was the coroner's duty to procure for the jury, if possible, an opportunity of seeing the body as it lay, and it was theirs to examine all its parts. Whether the coroner had been influenced by mere error or whether he had been actuated by a corrupt desire to pervert the course of justice it was their province to determine. At the conclusion of the judge's charge, the jury did not trouble to leave their box. There was a whispered conversation and then the foreman got to his feet.' We think the defendant is guilty but there is no proof that he received a bribe.' The judge was invited by the prosecuting counsel to adjourn the case and to release the defendant on bail.

In King's Bench prosecutions for misdemeanour, a convicted defendant only fell to be sentenced if and when the prosecutor moved for judgment, which he was not obliged to do. In November,1823 counsel appeared before the King's Bench to announce that the parties had come to terms. If the defendant resigned his coronership the prosecutors would not move for judgment. Resign he duly did and shortly afterwards a date was set for an election to fill the vacancy.

The fact that the special jury found no proof that a bribe had been received, does not mean of course that one was not offered? If, as Whitecombe claimed, he had never met Newton before the day of the inquest, what other explanation of his behaviour is there? Not that he honestly believed that death was due to natural causes, for after the inquest he admitted both to Vickers and to Coley that be believed Newton had killed his wife. It was certainly the prosecution's theory that a bribe had been offered. According to the farm servants, shortly after Whitecombe arrived at the Hall, he had sent for Newton and spent the next ten minutes closeted with him and, as the two of them left the room where they had been talking, Newton had been heard saying 'he hoped he would not make the worst of it and he would satisfy him in any degree.' This claimed the Crown was where the plan to screen and protect Newton was hatched. Significantly, his efforts on Newton's behalf did not end with the inquest. On the day of the latter's trial he spoke to Coley, who was at Shrewsbury to give evidence for the Crown, and urged 'We must do what we can to get him off.' Had the promised bribe not yet been paid and did Whitecombe fear that, if Newton was hanged, it never would be?

A question one inevitably asks is why the prosecuting magistrates were willing to allow Whitecombe to go unpunished. That a coroner convicted of corruption in office should escape without serving a day's imprisonment seems astonishing.[147] Their decision not to move for judgment appears to have gone unremarked in the press. It may be that their view, and indeed the view of the county, was that, the trial jury having found that no bribe had been paid, it was enough if Whitecombe was put out of office. There were certainly precedents for such lenity towards judicial delinquents. In 1805, Mr Justice Johnson, a judge of the Irish Court of Common Pleas, had been convicted in the English

---

[147] In *The Times* for 22 and 25 December 1823 it is wrongly stated that Whitecombe (described as coroner for Gloucestershire) was 'disgraced, fined and imprisoned.'

Court of King's Bench of criminal libel upon the Lord Lieutenant and Lord Chancellor of Ireland and upon a brother Irish judge. He was never sentenced; instead, after conviction, the Attorney General entered a *nolle prosequi* and the judge was allowed to retire on pension.[148]

With his resignation Whitecombe disappears from public view. The November edition of the *Salopian Journal* contained notices from candidates for the vacant office announcing their intention to stand in the forthcoming election,[149] and by the year end a successor had been appointed. Whether Whitecombe continued in the county practising as a surgeon or moved away is not known. Today, the opportunities for coroners to behave in the corrupt way in which he did are few and far between. Suspicious deaths are now the province of the police first and the coroner second. In 1926 it was enacted that a coroner must adjourn his inquest if notified that any person had been charged before an examining magistrate with homicide,[150] and in 1988 his power to commit for trial for homicide was abolished.[151] A relic of the days before police forces, it was seen as no longer serving any useful purpose.

---

[148] (1805) 29 How. St. Tr. 422.
[149] *Salopian Journal*, 26 November 1823.
[150] Coroners (Amendment) Act 1926.
[151] Coroners' Act 1988, s 11(6).

Dickens and The Bench

Stareleigh J, the short pompous judge, whom Dickens has presiding over the trial of *Bardell v Pickwick* was based on the Common Pleas judge, Stephen Gaselee,[152] whose mannerisms and eccentricities he had, in the opinion of the Temple, caught to a tee.[153] Gaselee's career at the bar and as a judge had been undistinguished: he never took silk and, on his elevation, had had to pay a hundred guineas to the son of a dead friend with whom he had, in his youth, laid 100 to 1 in guineas that he would never reach the bench. At the end of Hilary Term, 1837, a matter of months after the publication of the instalment of *The Pickwick Papers* which contained the trial scene, he resigned. The two events may have been unconnected; he was after all 75 years old when he retired; but many thought that Dickens' ridicule had driven him from the bench. Certainly, he left it without having completed the fifteen years' service necessary for a full pension.

Dickens is also credited with securing the dismissal of the Hatton Garden Stipendiary Magistrate, Andrew Laing.[154] By 1837 Laing was one of the longest serving of the London

---

[152] 1762-1837; appointed to the bench July 1, 1784; he died at 13, Montague Place, Russell Square, London on March 26, 1839.

[153] 'Dickens was generally thought to have caught exactly in *The Pickwick Papers*, the tones and mannerisms of Mr Justice Gaseless who was, indeed, very short and comically pompous and eccentric.' (Philip Collins, *Dickens & Crime*, 3rd edn, London 1994, p 82).

[154] Sir Thomas Skyrme, *History of the Justices of the Peace*, Chichester, 1991, vol ii, p. 4 'Dickens' oblique attack on Laing in *Oliver Twist* combined with a campaign mounted by the journal, *Figaro in London*, resulted in Laing's dismissal by the Home Secretary.'

stipendiaries.[155] A good lawyer and an accomplished scholar, he was a sour looking man, harsh towards prisoners and with a bad temper, which he rarely bothered to control. Serjeant Ballantine, who often saw him wending his way to the Athenaeum where he dined each day, says that he never saw him without being reminded of 'a shrivelled crab apple'.[156] Because of his manner of conducting proceedings he was much disliked and was often insulted in the street. He was also regularly attacked in the press especially by the satirical journal *Figaro in London*, which had promised its readers that it would not rest until it had secured his dismissal.

In 1837 *Oliver Twist* was being issued in monthly parts. On June 3 Dickens, who was working on the chapter in which Oliver is taken before a magistrate charged with theft, wrote to a reporter friend asking for his help:

> *'In my next number of Oliver Twist I must have a magistrate; and, casting about for a magistrate whose harshness and insolence would render him a fit subject to be shown up, I have as a necessary consequence stumbled upon Mr Laing of Hatton Garden celebrity. I know the man's character perfectly well; but, as it would be necessary to describe his personal appearance also, I ought to have seen him, which (fortunately or unfortunately as the case may be) I have never done. In this*

---

[155] Laing, Allan Stewart, born 1788, the son of James Laing of the Isle of Dominica in the West Indies; educated Trinity College, Oxford; BA 1809; MA 1812; called to the bar (Middle Temple) April 17, 1812; appointed stipendiary magistrate October 20, 1820; dismissed January 1838; after his dismissal he continued to live in the Temple; he died there (3 Tanfield Court) on February 12, 1862. According to Serjeant Ballantine, *Some Experiences of a Barrister's Life*, Richard Bentley & Son, London, 1883, p 53 'notwithstanding his unfortunate temper, he was a thoroughly honourable gentleman, a good lawyer and accomplished scholar.'
[156] Ballantine, p. 53.

> *dilemma it occurred to me that perhaps I might under your auspices be smuggled into the Hatton Garden office for a few moments some morning'.* [157]

The visit was arranged and Laing's place in literature thereby assured. Dubbed Fang, he is the magistrate before whom Oliver and Mr Brownlow are so ill-used. Everyone knew who was referred to and, as Dickens was at pains to stress, what was described was but 'a slight specimen of [Fang's] mode of administering justice'.

When Laing was dismissed the following year, many thought that the Home Secretary was, as Ballantine put it, following 'the lead of a popular author.' In fact, the incident which led to his removal occurred ten days' after Dickens' letter to the reporter, and not in the court-room but in the street.[158]

Around midnight on Tuesday, June 13, 1837 Dr Paine was walking along the Strand when, near to the junction with Catherine Street, he collided with Laing who was heading for his chambers in the Temple. He apologised. Laing, believing that Paine had run into him deliberately, flew into a rage and followed after him demanding to know his name. Paine would not give it. Laing called him 'a damned scoundrel' and began to belabour him with his umbrella. Paine grabbed hold of the umbrella and tried to take it from him. At this point a police officer appeared and Laing immediately instructed him to take Paine into custody for assault. The officer was reluctant to do so but, knowing who

---

[157] John Forster, *Life of Dickens*, London , 1874, Vol iii pp 4-5.
[158] See *The Times*, June 16 and December 11, 1837 and (1838) 2 JP p 26.

Laing was, felt he had no choice and took Paine off to Bow Street. There he was bailed to appear on the Wednesday morning.

On the Wednesday Paine duly answered his bail but, to everyone's surprise, Laing did not attend to substantiate the charge. The sitting magistrate caused enquiries to be made and it was then discovered that, on the Tuesday morning Laing, who had by now learnt that the man he had given into custody was a doctor, had signed the police sheet authorising his discharge without further inquiry. The Bow Street stipendiary immediately discharged Paine who requested and was granted an interview with Sir Frederick Roe, the chief metropolitan magistrate. At that meeting he made clear that, unless Laing apologised in open court for having given him into custody on a false charge and paid £5 to a charity of his choosing, he would sue. Laing sent word that he was willing 'to make every apology which could be considered due from one gentleman from another, provided it did not involve [an] admission of having acted wilfully in the wrong.' Paine immediately issued a writ claiming damages for assault and false imprisonment. On December 5, 1837, the day before the action was due to come on for trial, Laing consented to a verdict being entered against him for £50 damages and costs. The Home Office, which had been keeping a close watch on events, immediately wrote demanding an explanation from him, which he gave. On January 1st he was informed that the Home Secretary could not recommend his continuance in office. *Figaro in London* exulted. 'We have,' it boasted, 'frequently promised to be unwearied in our exertions to procure for society the boon of the dismissal of

Laing and, to this publication and to this alone, is the public indebted for the ferocities of Laing being exposed.'[159] No doubt, but it was Dr Paine who got him sacked.

William Ramshay[160]

In 1846, in an attempt to provide cheap local justice, Parliament created a new species of civil court – the county court. Grouped into circuits each presided over by a judge, the new courts were given jurisdiction over civil claims arising in their respective areas where the amount in dispute was £5 or less. The new judgeships carried a salary of £1,000 p.a. and only barristers were eligible for appointment.

In the second half of the nineteenth century the poor quality of the county court bench was the subject of frequent comment. 'The profession,' declared the *Law Times* in 1871 'has become thoroughly reconciled to the fact that any and every justification except learning and experience justify selection to the bench of the inferior court' with the result that 'from time to time men [are] appointed county court judges who not only [have] no reputation as lawyers but, worse still, [have] the reputation of being no lawyers.' Of those appointed a substantial number were 'men who had tried to make their way at the bar but without any significant

---

[159] Cited by Philip Collins, *Dickens & Crime*, 3rd edn, London, 1994.
[160] See *The Times*, June 5, August 22, 25, 27, September 9, 30, Oct 1, 2, 3, 7, 8, November 1, 18, 22, 26 and 27 1851; and F Boase, *Modern English Biography*.

results and probably saw the security of a judicial appointment as a more attractive proposition.'[161]

As well as being of indifferent ability, some of the early appointees proved remarkably accident-prone. In 1856, the judge of the Leeds court was successfully sued for libel at York Assizes.[162] In 1862 William Walker, the judge of the Sheffield Court came under attack from the local town council, a committee being appointed 'to inquire into the mode in which justice is done in the Sheffield county court.'[163] The differences between him and the Council were eventually smoothed over but the incident clearly took its toll, and the following year he resigned. Of the early appointees by far the worst was William Ramshay, whose conduct in office was such as to lead many, including *The Times*, to question his sanity and mental balance.[164]

When in April 1850 the judge of Liverpool county court drowned in the Mersey there was a good deal of speculation in the city as to who his successor would be. The appointment was in the gift of Earl of Carlisle as Chancellor of the Duchy of Lancaster. In May it was announced that the new judge would be

---

[161] 52 *Law Times* (1871) pp. 38 and 92. See also P Polden, *A History of the County Court*, CUP, 1999, pp. 51-52: 'My Aunt's Case' was for years the stock-in-trade of those who would sneer at county court justice. In a rural court...a defendant, having lost his cause, declared that he had no money to pay the debt but added that he believed his aunt would pay. 'Oh', said the judge, 'then I will make an order against your aunt.' *The Legal Observer*, giving the story wide currency, claimed 'we have heard of twenty judgments pronounced in these courts quite as absurd.' Incompetents could still be found in the twentieth century; in the 1960s Staveley Hill was reputed regularly to come into court armed with two books '*Everyman's Guide to the Law*' and *Ruff's Guide to the Turf*. Polden, p 245.
[162] The judge was TH Marshall, the plaintiff Barnett, a Leeds attorney, whom he had libelled in a pamphlet; 40s damages were awarded (F Boase, *Modern Biography*).
[163] *Sheffield Independent*, August 14 and October 11, 1862.
[164] Other nineteenth century county court judges whose conduct attracted severe public criticism included Vaughan Williams who, in 1885, agreed to resign after victimising a cabman with whom he had had a row in the street, and W H Cooke, in E Anglia, who drove suitors into the neighbouring district courts by his unpleasant ways. In 1868 a London judge had to suspend sittings because he was in gaol for debt. (Polden, op. cit., pp. 66 and 262).

Ramshay, a 44-year-old northern circuit barrister.[165] Few doubted that it was the fact that his father was the Earl's land agent that had won him preferment.[166]

It was an appointment which the Earl would soon have cause to regret. The new judge proved to be a man of explosive temper, given to insulting all who appeared before him. Witnesses and suitors, whom he took against, would be called fools and blockheads and accused of being drunk. To a city, which had resented his appointment from the start, such behaviour was like a red rag to a bull.

In Spring 1851, a memorial was sent to the Earl of Carlisle requesting that he remove Ramshay for misconduct and incapacity. It had been signed by no fewer than 3,500 people, including many from the local business community.

The Duchy office announced that the Earl would hold an inquiry into the allegations; until its outcome was known the judge would not sit, and deputies would be appointed to deal with the work of the court.

The inquiry opened at the Duchy Offices in London on June 3, 1851. Mr Whately QC and Mr Whitmore appeared for the memorialists, Serjeant Wilkins for Mr Ramshay. Some eleven

---

[165] William Ramshay, born c. 1814 at Brampton in Cumberland; 2nd son of Thomas Ramshay; educated at Trinity College, Cambridge; called to the bar (Inner Temple) Nov 28, 1833; between 1834 and his appointment to the bench he practised as a barrister on the Northern circuit from London chambers (Crown Office Row, Temple (1834-35); 24, Essex Court (1836); 18, Clements Inn (1837) and 2 Hare Court (1838-1850). Although he is described in the *Law List* as a special pleader and equity draftsman, it is clear that he also did criminal work; in 1841 he defended a bigamy case at Northumberland Assizes and in 1846 prosecuted a bigamist at Cumberland Assizes. His elder brother, Thomas, also practised on the Northern circuit for a short time; in the 1835 *Law List* he is shown as having chambers at 2, Gray's Inn Square. In the 1849 *Law List* there appears a third Ramshay, Robert E R, called to the bar by the Inner Temple the previous November.

[166] *The Times*, October 8, 1851 referred to the appointment as motivated by the Earl's wish 'to forward the son of an old client of his family.' Ramshay's grandfather had also been land agent for the Earl's family.

witnesses were called in support of the memorial, including two reporters from the *Liverpool Journal* who produced their shorthand notes. The thrust of their evidence was that the judge was a man of uncontrolled temper, whose general conduct and demeanour towards witnesses and suitors was discourteous and insulting. All were severely cross-examined. The inquiry was then adjourned until June 17 when witnesses were called in support of the judge, who claimed that his unpopularity was due to the fact that he was not a Liverpool man.

On August 20, the Earl announced his decision. On the evidence presented he did 'not feel himself called upon to remove [Mr Ramshay] from office.'[167]

Ramshay was jubilant. A wiser man might have congratulated himself on a narrow escape and have resolved to moderate his behaviour in future. But that was not Ramshay's way. He sent out invitation cards for a banquet to be held in the court building 'in honour of the great principle of judicial independence so long and so recklessly assailed in this town.' The dinner took place on September 20. In all some 40 guests attended, including the Liverpool stipendiary magistrate and the judge of the Cheshire county court. The mayor, however, did not, despite the judge 'in a carriage drawn by four grey horses with postilions waiting upon him with an invitation.' After dinner, Ramshay presented Serjeant Wilkins with a piece of plate and

---

[167] *The Times*, October 1, 1851 suggested that, had the inquiry not been held in London and had process been available to compel their appearance, more witnesses would have attended, and the outcome might have been different. Although the Earl declined to remove Ramshay he was, according to *The Times*, sufficiently persuaded of his unfitness for office 'as to engage to pay him a thousand a year for life rather than that he should continue in his office.'

launched into a long rambling speech in which he asserted that the death of his predecessor was due to persecution from the press of Liverpool. He was, he told his audience, determined to teach the press of Liverpool to behave themselves better, and assured them that the greater their insubordination the greater would be their punishment.[168] Serjeant Wilkins, in a speech of thanks, entreated Ramshay 'not to abuse the vantage ground he had gained,' told him that he could afford to forgive, and begged him, while he judged, to behave with mercy.[169] He might as well have saved his breath.

On September 27, a *Liverpool Journal* placard was posted on the court house wall. It read 'What Mr Ramshay thinks of the people of Liverpool.'[170] The sight of it threw Ramshay into a fury. On entering court, ignoring the list of cases waiting to be tried, he immediately despatched bailiffs to the offices of the *Journal* with instructions to bring the editor before him. The editor was Michael James Whitty, the retired chief constable of Liverpool and a man highly thought of in the town.[171] On learning the purpose of their errand, Whitty said them that he would accompany them if they had either a warrant for his arrest or a

---

[168] This was not the first time he had made such a threat. On August 25 at his first sitting in court since the enquiry he had talked of the need to make an example of those who had defamed and attacked him (*The Times*, August 27, 1851).
[169] *The Times*, October 1, 1851 (leader).
[170] It referred to a remark made by the judge that a witness in a case tried by him the previous day 'like many people in Liverpool, had no respect for the sanctity of an oath and was lacking in humanity.'
[171] Michael James Whitty; born in 1795 in Duncormick, County Wexford, Ireland;. editor of the *London and Dublin Journal* 1823-27 and of the *Liverpool Journal* 1829-33; Superintendent of the Night Watch, Liverpool Police, 1835; Chief Constable 1836; resigned on grounds of ill health 1843 (awarded a gratuity of £1000 by the Watch Committee and presented with silver tea service by the officers, clerks and constables of the force); purchased *Liverpool Journal* 1848; published *Liverpool Daily Post*, the first UK penny daily, 1855; known as 'the father of the penny press;' retired due to ill health 1872 and died the following year.

summons requiring his attendance. Informed that they had neither he sent them packing.

On learning that Whitty had declined to attend, Ramshay ordered the bailiffs to arrest him.[172] Back they went to the *Journal* offices, with reinforcements, and attempted to effect an arrest. Told that they still had neither summons nor warrant, Whitty instructed his staff to eject them and, after a scuffle, they were put out. The bailiffs turned to the police for help but they declined to assist in the absence of a warrant. Events now took a bizarre turn, Whitty's son, John, giving the Bailiffs in charge for assault. They were taken to the police station but by the time they got there, he had had a change of heart and elected not to press charges.

Upon hearing what had happened, Ramshay now condescended to issue a summons against Michael Whitty for wilfully insulting the judge and bailiffs in the execution of their duty contrary to s. 113 of the County Courts Act, 1846. Summonses were also issued against John Whitty for assault upon the bailiffs[173] and against the police officers who had taken the bailiffs into custody.

On Monday, September 30, Michael Whitty, accompanied by his solicitor Sir George Stephen, attended before the judge. Ramshay proceeded first to deal with the charge that Whitty had insulted him by causing the placard to be displayed outside the court. Having taken evidence as to its display, he brushed aside Sir George's submission that the words on the placard did not constitute an insult, announced that he found the charge proved

---

[172] This was something he had no power to do.
[173] Contrary to section 114 of the County Courts Act, 1846.

and fined Whitty £5 with seven days' imprisonment in default of payment.

He turned next to the charges of insulting and assaulting the bailiffs. In vain, did Sir George argue that, in the absence of an arrest warrant, the bailiffs had no right or power to arrest the editor. 'My instruction is equivalent to a warrant,' contended Ramshay. Announcing that he found the charges proved, he fined Whitty a further £5 for each offence, with seven days' imprisonment in default, the default sentences to run consecutively to each other.

Michael Whitty refused to pay the fines and, on Tuesday morning, he was arrested under a committal warrant and taken to Lancaster prison. At Lime Street railway station a large crowd gathered to wave him off. They cheered him to a man. Just as the train was about to depart, a railway official caused a gale of laughter by calling 'Any more gentlemen for Lancaster? Any more gentlemen for Lancaster Castle?' Whitty was not to be long at the Castle.

Meanwhile, back at the county court, the judge was proceeding to hear the charge against John Whitty. Sir George Stephen submitted on his behalf that his client had been perfectly justified in what he did, observing that if the bailiffs had come to his (Sir George's house) without warrant, without semblance of authority of any kind, as they did in this instance, he (Sir George) would have shot them through the head. At this those in the public seats burst into loud applause. The judge ordered the bailiffs to arrest the person responsible for the demonstration, threatening to fine them if they did not. 'But they all cheered,' protested the bailiffs. Eventually, a couple of those in the public seats were identified as having clapped and shouted and were fined £5 each. Ramshay now returned to the case of John Whitty whom he convicted and fined.

When the case against the police officers was called on, Ramshay announced that it would not be proceeded with 'in the interests of preserving good relations between the court and the police.'

Back in the business quarter, the money needed to pay the Whittys' fines was quickly raised and, by the Tuesday evening, Michael was heading back to Liverpool by train. A crowd of between 3,000 and 4,000, accompanied by a band, gathered at the station to greet him and when he alighted from the train he was loudly cheered. After making a speech of thanks, he was able, with difficulty, to extricate himself from his well-wishers and head for his home. Having given him a final cheer, the crowd marched to the county court where 'groans were given for the judge.'[174]

This time Ramsay had gone too far. It was by now not just the Liverpool newspapers which were calling for his removal. Describing his behaviour as outrageous, *The Times* demanded that the Earl of Carlisle take immediate action. 'The judge's removal,' it declared, 'is an absolute necessity.' [175]

In fact, a fresh memorial to the Earl had already been drawn up praying that he hold an enquiry, either in or near to Liverpool,

---

[174] *The Times*, October 3, 1851.
[175] *The Times*, October 8, 1851 (leader).

into the judge's recent conduct and calling for him to be removed on the grounds of both incapacity and misconduct.

A second enquiry was held, this time at Preston, on November 5, 1851. Despite the efforts of Serjeant Wilkins on the judge's behalf, the outcome was never in doubt and, on November 26, the Duchy Office announced that Ramshay had been removed. His successor was to be Mr Pollock, the judge of the Salford Hundred Court a gentleman who, according to *The Times*, was

> *remarkable for combining with dignity and firmness a courteous demeanour.*[176]

Never a man to take a reverse lying down, in January 1852 Ramshay applied to the Queen's Bench for leave to institute proceedings against Judge Pollock for usurpation of office, alleging that the Earl of Carlisle had acted unlawfully in removing him (Ramshay) from office. But the court would have none of it and dismissed his application, leaving him with a bill of £1,800 for legal costs.[177]

By July, 1853 he was dead.[178]

---

[176] *The Times*, November 27, 1851.
[177] See *Ex parte Ramshay* (1852) 18 QB 174.
[178] Polden, p 50 suggests that Ramshay was mentally ill. Certainly, he seems to have been convinced that the Liverpool press had driven his predecessor to his death, when the reality was that he fell from a ferry as it was making ready to dock and was drowned. In a letter to *The Times* published on October 6, 1851, Harden, the Cheshire county court judge who had attended the ill fated banquet, claimed that at the time of his appointment he had 'strongly advised [Ramshay] against attempting so laborious a duty in his enfeebled state of health.' See also (1851) 17 *Law Times*, p. 215 and 313.
No other county court judge was removed after Ramshay until Judge Bruce Campbell QC in 1983 (dismissed for smuggling – see *The Times*, December 6, 1983).

Death in Nottingham[179]

At around 10.30 p.m. on July 17, 1884, Mr Justice Watkin Williams,[180] who was in Nottingham to take the Assizes, died at a house in the town. A doctor and the police were called. Shortly afterwards the body was removed to the Judges' Lodgings, about half a mile away in High Pavement. There a *post-mortem* was carried out which established that death had been caused by a rupture of the aorta.

Officialdom took great pains to conceal the place and circumstances of death. The story put out by the Lodgings and published in the Nottingham newspapers was that, at around 8.30, the judge had gone for a walk and had later been found dead in his room. To ensure that nothing to the contrary emerged at the inquest, a person of 'high legal authority' (probably Lopes J, the senior assize judge) approached Mr Michael Browne, the borough coroner, and asked him to limit the evidence called to that necessary to prove identity and cause of death.

The inquest was held on July 19 in the dining room at the Lodgings. Once the jury had been sworn the coroner told them of the approach he had received. They indicated that they were content that the inquest follow the course which had been suggested.

---

[179] See *The Times*, July 19 and 21, 1884; *The Nottingham Evening Post*, July 19 and 21, 1884; *The Nottingham Daily Guardian*, July 18 and 21, 1884; *The Nottingham Journal*, July 19 and 21, 1884.
[180] Sir Charles James Watkin Williams born in 1828 was the eldest son of a Welsh clergyman. He was called to the bar in 1854 and took silk in 1873. From 1868 to 1880 he sat as MP for Denbigh. He was appointed a judge of the Queen's Bench Division in 1880. He was twice married. His first wife was the niece of Malins VC, his second the daughter of Lush LJ.

The coroner, however, was uneasy. He knew that there were rumours abroad in the town. 'There are,' he told the jury, 'circumstances connected with the death which I dare say most of you have heard of and which are of a very painful nature. It is no use blinking at the matter. It is well known that Sir Charles [Watkin] Williams died in a house in Nottingham.'

That death had taken place away from the Lodgings was put beyond doubt when Charles Field, the circuit butler, was called to give evidence of identity. 'I last saw [the judge] alive,' he said, 'about 8 o'clock in his room. I saw him next when he was brought [to the Lodgings] at about eleven o'clock.'

By the time the medical evidence had been gone through, the coroner, who had clearly been battling with his conscience since the inquest began, had reached a decision. He would not do what had been asked of him. It had, he declared, been his practice during the long time he had held the office of coroner never to make any distinction as to persons. 'Duke or chimney sweep' it made no difference as to the mode in which he conducted his inquiry. There must be evidence as to the circumstances of the death. 'There were other persons connected with the death whose characters were perhaps not worth a great deal, but still their characters were something and it would not be fair to let them go away [under] the slightest suspicion that they had done anything improper or likely to produce the death of the judge.'

Despite the protests of Mr. Aston, counsel for the family, the doctor was recalled. Questioned by the coroner, he revealed that the judge had died at 23, North Street. He explained that he had been called to the house by the householder, Mr Fish. Death had taken place only minutes before he arrived. The coroner then announced that he was going to call the girl. Mr Aston was on his feet at once. 'Do the jury think it necessary to go further now in the face of this evidence? I do appeal to the jury.' But the coroner insisted and into the witness box went Nellie Banks.

She said she had been with the judge when he died. He had made a noise in his breathing, had been given water and died minutes later. There had been no quarrelling or difference between them. What either of them was doing in the house she was neither asked nor explained. She added that it was Mrs Salmond who had sent for the doctor. Who Mrs Salmond was she did not say. With that, a verdict of death due to a rupture of the aorta was recorded.

All the local newspapers reported the inquest verdict but only the *Nottingham Journal* printed the evidence given. *The Times*, both in its obituary and its report of the inquest, spoke of the judge having been taken ill in the street and taken into a nearby house where he had died. But that was not the inquest evidence. If the judge's presence in the house could have been so easily and innocently explained it is inconceivable that it would not have been. Such explanation also begs the question what the judge was doing in North Street, a row of tradesmen's dwellings at the rear of Upper Parliament Street.

The truth of the matter and the reason for the attempted cover up is almost certainly that 23, North Street was a brothel and Nellie Banks a prostitute. Hence the coroner's reference to the painful circumstances attending the death, his slighting description of the character of those who were in no. 23 at the time and counsel's desperate attempt to stop Miss Banks being called. Nottingham certainly had no doubt. Within weeks of the death the following memorial card was circulating in the town:

In Memory of Mr Justice Watkin Williams
Who departed this life suddenly at Mrs. Salmand's,
Nottingham, Thursday Night July 17th 1884
Aged 56 years

In eight feet deep of solid earth
Sir Watkin Williams lies
He lost his breath, which caused his death
'twixt Nelly Blankey's (sic) thighs.[181]

---

[181] E Bryson, *A Portrait of Nottingham*, 3rd edn., Geo Hale, London, 1983, p. 196.

PART 3

PETTICOAT PERJURY

Will you hang him or marry him?

As late as the 1820s accusing a seducer of rape was seen as a way of bringing him to the altar. It was the course which the heroine of Richardson's novel *Clarissa* had been advised to take by her friend, Ann Howe.[182] Indeed, for a 'wronged woman' it was in reality her only means of redress, a civil suit for breach of promise of marriage being beyond the purse of most. And it was effective. Rape was, and until 1841 would remain, a capital offence, and, though the conviction rate was low, those convicted were normally 'left for execution.'

Complainants were often frank about their motivation. In 1827, an elderly spinster 'apparently the wrong side of forty' implored a London magistrate to compel the prisoner, whom she was accusing of raping her, to marry her. At Cork Assizes, in 1829, a coarse- mannered working woman made no bones about the reason why she had charged the accused with rape: 'He cracked my character and I expects compensation. [So would you] if you had a nice summer house and a fine tree growing in it and a ruffian cut it down so that it would not grow again.' Under questioning from the judge she admitted that she wanted to marry the prisoner.[183]

---

[182] S. Richardson, *Clarissa*, Penguin Books, 1985, Letter 317 at p 1017: '...it is my opinion that it would be very right for the law to oblige an injured woman to prosecute and to make seduction on the man's part capital, where his studied baseness and no fault in her will appeared. To this purpose, the custom in the Isle of Man is a very good one: 'If a single woman there prosecutes a single man for rape, the ecclesiastical judges empanel a jury; and it this jury finds him guilty, he is returned guilty to the temporal courts where, if he be convicted, the deemster, or judge, delivers to the woman a rope, a sword and a ring and she has it in her choice to have him hanged, beheaded or to marry him.'
[183] *R v. Murphy, The Times*, April 21, 1829

In England, compromises were most commonly struck at the committal stage. When, in 1805, Thomas Stapleton was brought before the Hatton Garden magistrate on a charge of attempted rape, he did not trouble to deny the accusation but immediately offered to marry the complainant and, the offer being accepted, he was held to bail 'until he shall fulfil his promise.'[184] Less impetuous prisoners waited to see what the complainant had to say in the witness box before making a move. If she showed no sign of backing down, then the nettle would be grasped and the magistrate asked to grant the prisoner permission to speak to her. The bargain was not always that the parties should wed; sometimes it was money not marriage that the prosecutrix was after. As Charlotte Rawlins said, in 1828, after accusing her master of rape, 'Is there not money to be got when a man behaves in this way to a young girl?'[185] Occasionally it was the magistrate who took the initiative. At Southwark Town Hall, in 1828, a charge of attempted rape against Thomas Taylor was abandoned when he and his accuser accepted the magistrate's forceful recommendation that he apologise and she drop the case.[186] Bargains struck after committal were rarer but not wholly unknown. In 1817 a grand jury at Hertford felt it had no option but to return 'no true bill' against three bargees accused of rape when it emerged that banns of marriage had recently been

---

[184] *The Times*, September 3, 1805.
[185] *R v. Thurtell*, *The Times*, August 20, 1829.
[186] *The Times*, October 3, 1828.

published between the actual supposed ravisher and the prosecutrix.[187]

In Ireland, the tradition was different. There compromises tended to be brokered at trial. If the parties had been on familiar terms prior to the alleged rape, it was a standard ploy for counsel to question the complainant about her present attitude towards and feelings for the prisoner. If it became clear that she was still fond of him she would be asked bluntly 'Would you rather hang him or marry him?' and if she answered 'Marry' that would be an end of the case. Indeed, it was not unknown for the judge to put the question himself, as happened in a trial at Cork in 1829 during which the complainant had been observed smiling at the defendant.[188]

Sometimes, the judge would take a more active role still. Those listening to the prosecutrix give evidence at the trial of Michael Maloney for rape at Limerick summer Assizes, 1824, could have had little inkling of how things would shortly turn out. She swore that she had been raped and could not be budged from her story. After she had left the witness box, defence counsel managed to elicit from another Crown witness that the parties had been due to be married just before the trial but that, because the accused was in custody, the priest had declined to officiate. The judge commented that confinement was no bar to a prisoner marrying; why, he remembered a rape case at Cork where the parties were married in the judge's room while the jury were out considering their verdict. Whether or not this anecdote had been

---

[187] *R v Stain, Tookey and Tookey*, The Times, March 8, 1817.
[188] *R v. Murphy* above.

intended as a hint, it was certainly taken as such. As soon as the jury had been sent out, a priest was fetched and the couple were married in the judge's chambers. This done, the jury were sent for and told that matters had come to the judge's notice which made it advisable for them to acquit the prisoner which they did. Although the procedure adopted was highly unusual (the case was reported in *The Times*[189] under the headline *Singular Termination of a Trial for Rape*), this was certainly not the only time it was employed. At Cork the following year, John Hearne, a well-to-do farmer, was acquitted of rape after marrying the prosecutrix in the judge's room, the split ring of the High Sheriff's watch chain being used as a ring. *The Times* reported that he left the court with his bride 'more in sorrow than in anger.'[190]

The appetite of the Irish bench for marriage-broking was not, however, unbounded. In another rape trial at the same Assizes[191] defence counsel, having failed to make any headway with the complainant, turned his fire on her mother. 'Had she any objection to her daughter and the prisoner marrying?' 'No,' she replied, 'but I fear they would not live happily together.' The jury took just fifteen minutes to find the prisoner guilty. After the verdict, the judge, Baron Pennefather, rose. By the time he came back into court a compromise had been hammered out which he was asked to approve. He refused. 'I will not countenance such trifling with justice,' he declared and proceeded to pass sentence of death.

---

[189] *The Times*, August 10, 1824.
[190] *R. v Hearne*, *The Times*, August 24, 1825 (reported under the headline *Irish Marriages*)
[191] *R v Callagan* *The Times*, August 25, 1825.

In the 1830s one hears no more of marriages in the judge's room and when, in 1841, rape became non-capital, the old stock question had to be put into retirement. Somehow 'Will you jail him or marry him?' did not have quite the same ring to it.

The Vicar's Daughter

The south Bedfordshire village of Harrold[192] lies on the Great Ouse some nine miles north west of the county town. At the time of Waterloo the vicar of this small sleepy place was Robert Woodward, a man in his early 50s.[193]

In the early evening of June 7, 1815 the Revd Woodward, accompanied by his two daughters, Susannah and Sarah, called on fellow cleric, William Hooper. This was no social visit. Hooper was a justice of the peace and they had come to report a rape upon Susannah.[194] It was a step which would have far reaching consequences for all three.

Upon learning the nature of their business, the magistrate sent for his clerk and proceeded to take Susannah's deposition. The story the pretty and heavily pregnant girl gave was this:

> *'On the evening of the 18th of October last between 6 and 7 o'clock in the evening, I was coming from the privy in my*

---

[192] It is mentioned in Domesday book and has a population of 1,300.
[193] Robert Woodward, born c. 1848, son of Robert Woodward, cleric of Oxford; educated at Brasenose College, Oxford; his family had Bedford connections, his grandfather Michael having had an estate at Salford in the county.
[194] According to *The Times* report, of the two girls, Susannah, who was 22 (the same age as Harris) was 'pretty and fair' but Sarah, who was three years older, had nothing prepossessing in either her manner or appearance.

> *father's garden, within a few yards of the house, the garden being overlooked by cottages, when James Harris, the son of the local saddler, sprang out and attacked me, placing a foot behind my legs, and throwing me down violently; the fall stunned me and during the time I lay senseless on the ground he effected his purpose; when I came to myself I shouted out and called for my sister, at which Harris produced a knife, held it to my throat and threatened to kill me. Soon after, my sister came out and pulled him off and he went away. As a result of [what he did] I am likely to become a mother.'*

It was not, she explained, the first time Harris had attacked her. In July last he had laid hold of her in the garden of her father's house. She had threatened to tell her father, but had agreed not to upon his promising not to repeat such behaviour.[195]

So far as the October incident was concerned her account was backed up to the hilt by her sister:

> *'On Tuesday the 18th October last, I was alone in the house; I heard the voice of my sister Susannah, calling out 'Sally' [from the garden] as if in great distress. I immediately ran into the garden and there saw my sister on the ground and a young man, named James Harris, a saddler of Harrold, holding her down upon the ground, with a knife in his hand close to her throat. I immediately cried out 'murder' and then Harris jumped up and, putting the knife close to my throat, said if I cried out he would run the knife into my throat. I said if he would remove the knife I would be silent. Harris then left the garden saying that if I told my father, he or somebody else would kill me or my sister.'*

The two girls were highly respectable but it was a curious story. Why had they not complained at the time? When had the vicar first realised his daughter was pregnant and what

---

[195] During the taking of her deposition Susannah explained that at the time of the rape it was dark. At this the vicar interrupted 'No, my dear, it was a fine moonlight night.' How did he know?

explanation had she given him? Surely he must have known long before June?

While taking the girls' deposition, the magistrate noticed how at times the vicar had tried to prompt Susannah: when she explained that it was dark at the time of the rape, he immediately corrected her and yet how did he know?

Whatever his personal doubts or misgivings, the Rev Hooper felt obliged to issue a warrant for Harris' arrest and when the youth was brought before him later that day, despite his protests of innocence, he committed him in custody for trial at the Assizes.

He was tried in 1816 at Bedford Spring Assizes and acquitted. The sequel was another Assize prosecution – this time of the vicar and his two daughters for conspiring falsely to accuse Harris of rape. Their case came on at Lent Assizes, 1817.[196] According to *The Times*, it produced

> *'an uncommon degree of interest in all parts of the county...the court was crowded from an early hour with persons of all rank.'*

Serjeant Blossett, opening the prosecution case to the jury, stressed that the accused stood charged with conspiring to take the life of an innocent man. After outlining the facts, he observed that if the charge against Harris was false, the daughters must be guilty for both had been party to making it; as for the father, it was inconceivable that Susannah should have lived under his roof for so many months without making disclosure, or without his

---

[196] The trial judge was Mr Baron Graham. Serjeant Blossett, who had defended Harris upon his trial, appeared for the prosecution; the accused were represented by Mr Hunt.

making enquiry about her condition and yet it was only when it became impossible to conceal her condition any longer, that he took her before the magistrate.

The Crown's evidence was brief. Their main witnesses were Harris and the Rev Hooper.[197] Harris, although he stoutly denied having had sexual intercourse with Susannah, was not especially convincing. When examined in chief he claimed that he had no acquaintance with the Rev. Woodward, except when he went to school with him for a year between 13 and 14. This was his only acquaintance with him and he had none whatever with his daughters. In cross-examination, however, he was forced to admit that he had in fact had contact with the family and with Susannah in particular: it was true that that he had many times fetched the newspaper from Mr Woodward's and returned it afterwards; on one occasion he had played the flute at a party at the vicarage;[198] he had paid addresses to the Woodward's servant girl and on one occasion he had accompanied Miss Susannah on the road towards Olney.[199]

---

[197] The Crown also called Ann Robinson, who told the jury that long before the fact of her pregnancy was publicly known Susannah had appeared ill and taken to wearing a large cloak. She was followed into the witness box by Elizabeth Glenton who, after much prompting and cajoling, was eventually induced to relate how she had been approached by Mr Woodward who wanted her to say that she had heard her apprentice say that he was with Harris when he was with Woodward's daughter. 'Did you hear him say that?' she was asked. 'No,' she replied and promptly fainted. She was carried out of court, leaving defence counsel to bemoan the fact that he had not had the chance to cross-examine her. It was suggested by defence counsel to the constable who had arrested Harris that Mr Woodward had been told that the case would be dropped if he gave up his living, but the constable denied this.

[198] He denied, however, that he saw either young lady on this visit; he stood behind a door and played when Mr Woodward rapped on the door.

[199] She was, he said, on a pony but was afraid to ride it and so he took it back to Horring while she went on to Olney in a chaise.

The three accused, being incompetent in law to give evidence in their own defence (as had been Harris at his trial),[200] at the close of the Crown's case, Mr Hunt, counsel for the defence, rose to address the jury. Harris' acquittal, he told them, should not be taken as reflecting any discredit upon Susannah. It was due solely to the fact that she had not made prompt complaint, which in law was fatal to the case against him.[201] The only evidence against the accused was that of Harris, and he had been anything but frank in the witness box. The two girls on the other hand were young women of high character. As for the father, what were the grounds upon which his guilt was supposed to rest? Why forsooth that his daughter could not have been eight months' pregnant in his house without his knowledge.

> *'Good God. Could anything be more absurd than this? Was a father who had brought his children up in the strictest paths of virtue, to be watching them with suspicion and to be viewing them as common prostitutes? Could any parent who loved and confided in his offspring, harbour a suspicion so foul that they would prostitute themselves in the way in which they must have done to produce the appearance described? Of all men living, a father ... was the last man who would have made such a discovery. What was Mr Woodward's conduct when he did find out what had happened? Did he not immediately carry his daughters before a magistrate? What else could he have done to show his indignation?'*

Any effect this speech produced upon the jury was quickly dispelled by the judge's summing up. Harris had been acquitted of rape, he told the jury, not on a point of law but on the merits; if

---

[200] As to the incompetency rule see further p. 128 below.
[201] Hunt alleged that as soon as Susannah Woodward had gone through her testimony, Serjeant Blossett had got up and told the jury that by a rule of evidence, which had been made a rule of law, [Harris] must be acquitted.

the complainant had been raped, it was highly improbable that she would not have told her parent or that she did not know that she could be protected against the defendant's threatened violence. 'I was,' he told the jury

> *'most anxious for the sake of this unfortunate family, that something would occur which would lessen the enormity of their guilt…It is with pain, however, that I am driven to say no such circumstance has transpired.'*

The jury needed no further hint and, after a few minutes' consultation, found all three accused guilty. The vicar was sentenced to two years' imprisonment in the county gaol, the daughters to twelve months.

According to *The Times*, their fate excited but very little commiseration in the county.

Who had got Susannah pregnant? The judge in his summing up suggested that, even if he did not rape her, Harris might well have been the father of her child. That would, of course, explain his false denial that he knew or had had any contact with the Woodward girls. It would also explain why Susannah had pointed the finger at him? Given the difference in their rank it is unlikely that she would have wished to marry Harris or that her father would have allowed her do so. But, as the date of confinement approached, the need to proffer some explanation of her condition, which did not reflect on the family, became daily more urgent. In Victoria's day the solution often adopted by genteel families in such situation was to send the girl away to a laying-in house in London to have her child, and then have it adopted. But that was an option probably not open to the Woodwards. Instead, the decision was made to charge Harris with rape. To lay a false charge which could end up costing the accused his life was monstrous behaviour on the part of a man of the cloth, but at least intelligible if he was the seducer. One wonders if the truth of the matter is that, when the father taxed Susannah with her pregnancy, she not only named Harris but, to divert her father's wrath, claimed that he had raped her.

What happened to the child Susannah was carrying or to the Woodwards after their release from prison we are not told. Did they move or emigrate? Did they, perhaps, try and support themselves by teaching, with the girls taking positions as governesses in places which news of the scandal had not reached? We shall never know.

The Trials of Henry Hatch

Had he been prepared to tender an apology to the parents of the two girls whom he was accused of indecently assaulting, the Rev. Henry Hatch would have avoided prosecution. But he would not do so: the matter was one of principle. His conviction by an Old Bailey jury and the further legal proceedings to which it gave rise, excited huge public interest: overnight he became a household name. They also led to calls for reform of the law of criminal procedure and evidence.

Born in 1817, Henry John Hatch was the son of an Anglican vicar.[202] Educated at Eton and Cambridge, in the 1840s he went out to New South Wales where he worked for a time as a tutor. In 1845 married a woman seven years his junior. After the wedding he returned to England with his new wife and began to study for the Church. Following his ordination in 1848 he was offered and took a curacy in Staffordshire. In 1851 he was appointed chaplain to the Wandsworth House of Correction, a post which carried a salary of £250 a year, with living accommodation thrown in.

In 1856, he and his wife, having no children of their own, took under their wing a five-year-old orphan, named Lucy Harriet, whom they treated as their *de facto* adopted child. In the summer of 1859, in an attempt to boost their income, they advertised for boarding pupils. A Wiltshire couple, named Plummer, who had two young daughters replied to the advertisement.

On July 11, Mrs Plummer, accompanied by her elder child, Eugenia, called on the Hatchs. The upshot of the visit was that it was agreed that the Hatchs should take both girls at a fee of £50 per child per year. Hatch immediately engaged a young woman, named Howe, as governess for the children.

On August 11, Mrs Plummer and Eugenia made a second visit to Wandsworth. This time Mr Plummer was with them. They made a thorough inspection of the house, paying particular attention to Hatch's study which, during the day, was to serve as the schoolroom. Mrs Plummer told the Hatchs that Eugenia was

---

[202] His father was vicar of Walton on Thames.

used to being petted, and had been in the habit of getting into the bed of her former schoolmaster. Mrs Hatch replied that Lucy was allowed into their bed and she had no objection to Eugenia doing the same. At 7 pm the parents said their farewells to Eugenia and left. After their departure the child appeared out of sorts and, in an attempt to cheer her up, Hatch ran into the front garden telling Lucy and Eugenia to chase him. The three of them remained out in the garden playing chase until tea time. Their play had been observed from the front window by Mrs Hatch, Miss Howe, the governess, and two young French women who were staying at the house.

On August 25, the Plummers called again. This time Stephanie, their younger child, was with them. In the two weeks since she had last seen her parents Eugenia had, if what she was later to say was the truth, been repeatedly sexually abused. The newspaper reports of Hatch's trial give scant detail of the nature of the abuse, merely observing that the particulars were 'unfit to be reported.' But this much can be pieced together: she was claiming that she had been touched indecently while in the Hatchs' bed, and that Hatch had also come into her bedroom at night and assaulted her. In all, she had been the victim of at least five sexual assaults, the first of which had taken place in the front garden on the day of her arrival. If that was true, it meant that Hatch had begun to abuse her almost as soon her parents were out of the door, and had behaved indecently with her in front of his wife. If anything had been going on, her parents' visit on the 25th provided her with an opportunity to complain, but she said nothing.

The Plummers would later claim that, just before they left, as she was being taken to the closet by her mother, Eugenia burst into tears and begged to be taken home. But her tears and entreaties produced no effect and the parents departed, leaving both girls in the Hatchs' care.

The following morning they were back. On entering the house, Mrs Plummer saw Lucy playing in the hallway while her own daughters were busy at their books. She complained that this was favouritism and announced that she was taking the girls away. The thunderstorm which there had been overnight had, she said, been a judgment on her for leaving them and she had come to take them home. According to Hatch, she also said that the children were not treated as she wished and was particularly aggrieved that 'a child who was an heiress to £15,000' had been made to sleep on calico sheets. Mrs Plummer would later claim, in the witness box, that the reason she returned on the 26th was because she felt that something was not right. Be that as it may, her parting from the Hatchs was cordial enough. She and her husband dined with them before they left for Paddington for their train. As she was leaving, Mrs Plummer gave Lucy a Noah's Ark and 5s and, according to Hatch, talked of placing the children with him again after Christmas. This cordiality was despite the fact that, while the children's clothes were being packed, Eugenia had told her mother that Hatch was a disgusting man who had behaved indecently to her. Both parents were to say that when she first made the allegation, they did not credit it but when, on the way back to Wiltshire, the girl went into detail they decided that something must be done.

The next morning they were attended by their solicitor, Mr Pratt, who took written statements from both girls. Mr Plummer then consulted London solicitors. On their advice, he wrote a letter of complaint to the Bishop of Winchester setting out the children's allegations. The Bishop wrote to Hatch, informing him what was being alleged against him, and to the visiting magistrates at Wandsworth prison asking them to conduct an investigation. Before the date set for the hearing before the magistrates, Hatch resigned his chaplaincy thereby depriving them of jurisdiction. He would later give as his reason that Onslow, the prison governor, had advised him that, even if the charges were dismissed, his position at Wandsworth would be untenable. Resignation was a grave step to take. His salary was Hatch's only source of income and the house, which went with the chaplaincy, his only accommodation. He sought no advice from colleagues or clergy about his position, but simply left home and went into lodgings in Poplar. His reason for keeping quiet about the allegations was, apparently, that he hoped the matter would be hushed up.

In the meanwhile, upon learning that the hearing before the visiting magistrates would not now take place, Pratt, the Plummers' solicitor, attended at the Wandsworth magistrates' court and obtained a warrant for Hatch's arrest. Armed with the warrant, he approached Mrs Hatch suggesting that it would be in everyone's interest if a meeting could be arranged between himself and her husband. A meeting took place a few days later at *Ridler's Hotel*, Holborn. Pratt, who attended accompanied by a policeman, told Hatch that if he admitted that the girls' allegation were true and apologised the matter would go no further. This he refused to do adding, according to Pratt, 'I must have been mad.' He asked the officer what the charges were and what the punishment for such offences was. He was told that the magistrates could sentence him to six months' with hard labour for each offence. Having turned down Pratt's offer, he was then arrested under the warrant and taken before the Wandsworth stipendiary magistrate.

On November 14, there was a preliminary hearing which lasted some three hours. A number of defence witnesses were called including those who had seen the game of chase in the garden. At the conclusion of the evidence, the magistrate, observing that the case was one of importance which merited investigation before another tribunal, committed Hatch for trial at the Old Bailey. He bailed him in his own recognisance of £500 with two sureties of £250 each. Hatch was, however, unable to find the necessary sureties and so had to stay in custody. Despite the problems over bail he was able to obtain top class representation, his solicitors being Lewis & Lewis and his counsel the vastly experienced Serjeant Ballantine.

His trial came on at the December Sessions before Baron Bramwell. The indictment contained two counts of indecent assault and several counts of common assault. The prosecution case was that on August 11, while he was in the garden with Eugenia and Lucy, he had put Eugenia's hand into one of his trouser pockets which had a hole in it; that he had touched her indecently on the night of a party in August; that on almost every night while she was staying under his roof he had gone into her bedroom and indecently assaulted her; that on a number of mornings he had taken Eugenia into his bed, while his wife was up and washing, and had behaved indecently towards her, and that he had indecently assaulted Stephanie in bed.[203]

The principal witnesses for the prosecution were the two girls. According to *The Times* report of the trial, both gave their evidence in 'a simple and artless manner' and, although they were both subjected to a severe cross-examination, 'very little was elicited which [tended] in any way to invalidate their testimony.' The accused and his wife were by law incompetent to give evidence in his defence but the witnesses, who had given evidence for the defence at the preliminary hearing, were available to be called. Ballantine decided, however, merely to call evidence as to Hatch's good character. His reason for taking this course was, almost certainly, to avoid giving the Crown the last word with the jury (if the defence called only character witnesses they had the right to the final speech; if, however, they called witnesses as to fact it was the Crown who had the last word). His speech to the jury was extremely powerful. The two girls, he argued, had trumped up the charges as a means of getting themselves taken away from a school which they did not like. He

---

[203] *Hatch v Lewis* (1861) 2 F & F 467 at pp 470-71.

stressed the accused's impeccable character, and argued against probability of man with such a character having committed such offences; he categorised as wholly incredible the claim that the accused had embarked on a campaign of indecency which had begun within minutes of the girls' parents departing on the 11th and had continued after that in front of his wife. Bramwell B, in his summing up, made the same point. But it cut no ice with jury. After 50 minutes' retirement, they returned with verdicts of guilty on both counts.

As he was led away to begin a four year sentence, Hatch protested that he was absolutely innocent, said that the two girls had told abominable lies and predicted that a time would come when his innocence would be proved.

But how was this to be done? A man convicted of a criminal offence by a jury had at this time no right of appeal against the verdict. The only course open to him was to petition the Home Office for a pardon. To this end, his solicitors busied themselves taking statements (which were then reduced to the form of statutory declarations)[204] from Hatch and his wife (who had both been legally incompetent to testify as his trial), and from the witnesses present at the Old Bailey whom Ballantine had decided not to call. The trial jury were approached and, after reading the statements, eleven of them declared that if, at the time of the trial, they had been aware of the facts deposed to, they would not have convicted the accused. The Home Office response was that for Hatch to be granted a pardon nothing short of a conviction of the

---

[204] A statement which the person making it solemnly declares to be true before a commissioner for oaths or magisterial officer.

complainants for perjury would do. Although both the Plummer girls had given evidence at trial, Hatch's solicitors decided to direct their fire at the elder girl. But, if Eugenia was to be put on trial, either a magistrate must be persuaded to commit her for trial, or committal proceedings by-passed and application made to grand jury direct for an indictment against her. If the latter course was to be followed, the defence would have to obtain the leave of a High Court judge to prefer an indictment. An application for leave was duly made and, as chance would have it, listed before Bramwell B, who had been the judge at Hatch's trial. He granted leave.

So Hatch now had leave to prosecute the young girl but that still left the question of how a prosecution was to be financed? It was decided to launch an appeal fund and an advertisement was placed in *The Times* soliciting subscriptions. The advertisement stated that the jury which tried Hatch had repented his conviction and leave had been obtained to prosecute for perjury, this being only remedy in absence of a right of appeal in criminal cases. Much was made the fact that the allegations of the two girls were uncorroborated, of the fact that Hatch was of good character and of the dangers, which all would be subject to, if convictions could be obtained upon such evidence. The advertisement, which was almost certainly a contempt of court as tending to prejudice pending criminal proceedings, drew a sharp retort from the Plummers' solicitors in the correspondence column of *The Times*.

A bill of indictment having been duly obtained from a grand jury,[205] Eugenia's case came on for trial in the No 1 court at the Old Bailey on May 9 before two judges, Mr Baron Channell and Mr Justice Keating.[206] The young girl was brought into court by her father and allowed to sit next to her solicitor, instead of in the dock. Different counsel appeared than at Hatch's trial. The flamboyant Edwin James QC (only weeks away from disbarment)[207] was brought into lead for the prosecution, whilst, for Eugenia, Serjeant Shee appeared with two junior barristers.

The major difference between the two trials was, however, that this time it would be Eugenia's, not Hatch's, mouth which would be shut. He and his wife, incompetent to give evidence at his trial, were fully competent against her. A true turning of the tables.

Edwin James, in opening the case to the jury, stressed its importance to Hatch and the improbabilities of the story told by girl. Her evidence at the original trial was read out to the jury, after which he called as his first witnesses Hatch and his wife.

---

[205] A prosecutor seeking to indict an accused had to go before a grand jury at the court of trial, with his witnesses, and satisfy them that there was sufficient evidence against the accused to justify indicting him; if the grand jury was satisfied it would mark the indictment 'true bill' and the accused would be tried upon it; if not so satisfied, they would mark it 'no true bill' and the accused would be discharged.

[206] At the start of the century, when the Old Bailey had only one courtroom, it had been usual for the two common law judges who came to deliver Newgate gaol to sit together; as the one presided over a trial, his brother would be reading the papers for the next case in the list. As court room accommodation increased (by 1860 the Old Bailey had four courtrooms), this practice had been given up and the common law judges would sit in separate courts. The fact that two judges presided at Eugenia's trial shows how important it was thought to be.

[207] He was disbarred on July 18 (the charges found proved against him by the Benchers of his Inn were (i) for his own benefit involving the son of Lord Yarmouth in debts amounting to £35,000; (ii) obtaining £20,000 from a solicitor by misrepresentation; and (iii) borrowing £1250 from the defendant in an action in which he was counsel for the plaintiff on the pretence that he would go easy on him in cross-examination). After his disbarment he went to America and was admitted to the New York bar. He returned to England in 1872 and the following year was articled to a London solicitor. He died in 1882.

They roundly denied the girl's accusations. They were adamant that it was Mrs Plummer, who had asked that Eugenia be allowed to come into their bed, and that both she and Stephanie had had ample opportunity to complain to her parents or to the governess before they were taken away, but had not done so. Mrs Hatch said that she had watched her husband playing in the garden on the 11th and would have seen any indecency, had there been any, as would those who were with her, but no-one did. She denied that her husband had ever behaved indecently whilst Eugenia was in their bed, and insisted, as he had, that child was only allowed under the counterpane not under the sheets. The governess, Hatch's mother-in-law, two young French women and Lucy, the Hatchs' eight-year-old, were called to confirm that there had been no indecency during the game of catch on the 11th. The governess said that Eugenia had never made complaint to her and that she had always appeared happy. Hatch's solicitor was called to say that the witnesses, from whom the jury had heard, had all be in attendance at his trial but had not been called at Ballantine's insistence.

Serjeant Shee, in opening the defence case, commented that, if the witnesses, who spoke as to the garden incident were telling the truth, it was astonishing they had not been called at the original trial. Also, he asked how could children as young as this, who had been religiously brought up, know of the things which they had spoken to.

If Eugenia could not be called, Stephanie could and was. She repeated the evidence she had given at Hatch's trial, that he had come into her bedroom at night and indecently assaulted her, but added that her bedroom door was open and that Mrs Hatch was outside, less than ten feet away and in a position to see what her husband was doing. This evidence caused a sensation in court. If she was telling the truth, the wife was an accomplice. If Stephanie's testimony was damaging to her sister, the evidence of the mother was worse.

In cross-examination, Edwin James quickly established that the two girls had not been given a religious upbringing, Mrs Plummer conceding that she did not take them regularly to church but insisting that neither she nor they were any the worse for that. Asked about their school attendance, she admitted that Stephanie had never been to any school before the Hatchs' and could not read or write; as for Eugenia, she had been to some eight or ten schools but had not stopped at any of them long; in one year she had been taken away from three schools in Bath, but there had been a good reason in each case and, in any event, 'a change was good for her.' By the end of the case she had been shown up as a buffoon. At one point she startled everyone in court by the loudness of her answer, only to explain 'I like to answer firm.' No, she said, she had not been drinking brandy and water before she came into court; that was yesterday. Today she had been drinking sherry wine. She accepted that on August 25 and 26, on the way back to Paddington from the Hatchs', she had taken beer and had sent out for stout when Hatch was convicted.

When her husband took her place in the witness box, he was soon in difficulty. Having told the jury that he was owner of considerable estate, he was asked by Edwin James whether it was true that no servant would live in with him and wife because of his wife's behaviour. He said that he did not think so but agreed that it might be so. He agreed that he had had to pay £5 to a servant who had complained of his wife's treatment of her. 'Did she not hit her with a poker?' he was asked. 'No, it was with a candlestick,' came the reply.

No doubt, Serjeant Shee would have liked to make a closing speech to the jury to try and undo some of the damage done but, having called evidence, he was not entitled to. The last word went to Edwin James and he did not waste it. Having stressed that for his client Eugenia's acquittal would mean ruin whereas for her it would mean only trifling punishment, he proceeded to rehearse the evidence against her.

On Saturday 12 (the fourth day of the trial) Mr Baron Channell summed up.[208] He told the jury that the case was a difficult one in which he could offer them no assistance. He stressed that if the accused girl's claims were true Mrs Hatch must be an accomplice in her husband's alleged crimes. The jury retired to consider their verdict at 5.45 p.m. They returned at 8 p.m. with a guilty of verdict, coupled with a strong recommendation of mercy. Announcing that he wished to consult with Mr Justice Keating on the question of sentence, the judge adjourned the case until Monday and enlarged Eugenia's bail.

On the Monday the young girl surrendered to custody and was put in the dock. According to the reporters present, she did

---

[208] His summing up took 7 ¾ hours.

not appear to exhibit any concern at her position. Having observed that perjury was a very serious offence, the judge said that his impression was that she had told the false story originally for the purpose of being taken away from Mr Hatch's and not being sent back. He wanted to deal with her as leniently as he could but perjury was a serious offence. The sentence was that she be imprisoned in Holloway for three weeks, and that she then be sent to a reformatory school for two years, but added that the authorities might well lift the latter part of the sentence if satisfied that proper arrangements had been put in place for her upbringing and education.

On May 21 Hatch was granted a free pardon and released from Newgate. Four weeks later came an announcement that Eugenia had also been pardoned on the condition that she be placed in the care of a lady, who had been selected by her friends.

Anyone who supposed that this was an end of the matter was quite wrong. There was another instalment yet to come. It was Hatch's belief that, had the witnesses, who were waiting to give evidence at his trial, been called to testify he would never have been convicted, much less have had to languish in gaol as a convicted prisoner, a particularly humiliating situation for a former prison chaplain. For this state of affairs he blamed his lawyers and he wanted blood.

In November 1860, he commenced an action in the Court of Exchequer against Lewis & Lewis claiming damages for negligence.[209] They had not, he alleged, either before or during

---

[209] Hatch v Lewis (1861) 2 F & F 467; 7 Jur NS 1085.

his trial, used due care and skill in preparing and conducting his defence; in particular, they had not taken proper instructions as to witnesses, had not properly instructed counsel at the trial and had taken no pains to call the witnesses, who could have given evidence on his behalf. Had they done so he would not have been convicted and, because of their negligence he had been incarcerated, had suffered damage to his reputation and had been put to the expense of prosecuting Eugenia. He put his loss at £5,000.

He was on a difficult wicket from the start. To have any hope of recovering more than nominal damages, he had to prove not only that Lewis & Lewis had been negligent but also that, but for their negligence, he would have been acquitted. Had he been able to show that they were to blame for his witnesses not being called, he might have stood a chance of success. But they were not. In a conference with Ballantine in prison Hatch had said that he would be guided by counsel as to what evidence should be called at trial, and Ballantine went into the witness box and said, in terms, that it had been his decision and his decision alone not to call witnesses, he being strongly of opinion that calling them would be unwise. After this testimony, the case was as good as lost and, although the jury found for Hatch (presumably because they found that the solicitors to have been at fault in some respect), they awarded him only 40s damages. This was a Pyrrhic victory, indeed, for it meant that court could refuse him his full costs, on the grounds that the action should have been brought in the county court, which is what it did. Still Hatch would not give up and instructed his lawyers to move for a new trial. They did and lost, leaving him with yet more costs to pay.

Having exhausted his legal remedies, Hatch now disappeared from public view. In 1866 he was appointed chaplain to the Maidstone Poor Law Union and in 1867 rector of Stanbridge in Essex. From 1888 to 1895 he was vicar of Little Linford in Buckinghamshire. He died on October 6, 1898, aged 77.[210]

His case demonstrated how unsatisfactory was the rule of evidence which prohibited a prisoner and his spouse giving evidence in his defence. As Pitt Lewis, the author of the leading textbook on the law of evidence, observed in a letter published in *The Times* on May 18, 1861.

> *'The verdict of the jury (which tried Eugenia Plummer) was diametrically opposed to that pronounced by the (jury which tried the Revd Hatch). No man can blame either jury but both were placed in a most unfair position. Each had been forced by law to decide on what was practically an ex parte statement [i.e. on evidence from one side only].*[211]

---

[210] According to *Alumni Cantabrigenses* he was also the editor and proprietor of *The Philanthropist*. He was the author of three books *John Mildred, Pagleston Oyster* and *Logs for the Christmas Fire*.

[211] Cf O'Hagan QC in a Lecture to the Juridical Society reported at (1857) 29 LT 146:

> A fight took place between two factions coming home from a fair. Informations and cross-informations were sworn with the very object of including among the accused such individuals as could give evidence for the defence. 'The Ryans' ... were the first put upon their trial. Their opponents, the 'Carrolls' came to the table one after another and told one side of the story. Where their evidence closed, the case closed. The jury then retired to consider their verdict and then what occurred? The Carrolls all walked into the dock to take their trials before a new jury, and the Ryans walked out of it for a time in order to be examined as witnesses. The new jury heard a new case. Each jury was forced to decide upon one-sided evidence.'

Over the next 30 or so years Parliament chipped away at the rule, but it was only in 1898 that the law granted all accused persons the right to give evidence and to call their spouses in their own defence.

The rule prohibiting appeals in criminal cases survived even longer, only being finally reversed in 1907.[212] It, of course, remained open to any aggrieved prisoner to take the course that Hatch had done, but prosecuting witnesses for perjury was an expensive business well beyond the means of most who passed through the criminal courts. Over the next few years one finds occasional instances of such prosecutions but they were few and far between.[213]

---

[212] By the Criminal Appeal Act, 1907 which established a Court of Criminal Appeal.
[213] In 1866 the Home Office advised a prisoner who was alleging that he had been wrongly convicted of rape to proceed as Hatch had done (R v Toomer, *The Times*, 5 September 1866 (leader); for another example of its employment see R v Kinnear, *The Times*, 22-27 August, 1872; as to the expense see *The Times*, 3 September 1866 (letter).

PART 4

GALLOWS TALES

Going to see a man hanged

The London mob enjoyed executions and in the eighteenth century flocked to Tyburn hangings in their thousands. To minimise obstruction to traffic and the risk of public disorder, the city authorities in 1783 transferred executions from Tyburn to Newgate. Over the next quarter century most county towns followed suit, abandoning traditional execution sites in favour of a portable scaffold erected outside (or in some cases on the roof) of the county gaol.[214] The change did not diminish popular enthusiasm for the spectacle. In 1807 the crowd outside Newgate at the hanging of Holloway and Heggarty was so immense that 30 spectators were crushed to death just before the drop fell.[215]

In the country zest for executions was no less keen.[216] On a hanging day country people would swarm into the county town from neighbouring towns and villages, some having walked very long distances indeed: in 1823, 40,000 people, of whom a good proportion had come down from London, saw Thurtell hang at Hertford.[217] At an execution outside the shire hall Nottingham in 1844 the crowd was so dense that twelve people, mostly women and children, were trampled to death.[218]

---

[214] Gaols where executions were carried out on the roof included Derby, Horsemonger Lane in London, and Shrewsbury.
[215] In 1831 21 people had to be treated at nearby St Bartholomew's Hospital after a barrier broke at the execution of Bishop and Warren (both were 'burkers').
[216] If robbed of their sport crowds could turn ugly; when, in 1801, Basil Montagu obtained a reprieve for two men who were due to be executed for sheep stealing, he was strongly advised by the High Sheriff of Huntingdon to leave the town as speedily and privately as he could to avoid ill treatment from 'the disappointment he had occasioned.'
[217] Thurtell had brutally murdered his erstwhile gambling companion, John Weare.
[218] Gibbetings were almost as great a draw as hangings: in April 1792 some 40,000 people waited all day on Attercliffe Common, Sheffield to see Spence Broughton's body gibbeted.

After 1815, owing to the repeal of capital statutes, the number of executions fell steadily. The size of the crowds attending, however, grew. This was due in part to the coming of the railways. When the notorious murderer Rush was hanged at Norwich in 1849 trainloads travelled down from the metropolis to watch.[219] But for the railways the execution at Stafford in 1856 of Palmer, the Rugeley Poisoner, would never have attracted the huge crowd it did, for all the culprit's notoriety.[220] In April 1857 several hundred people travelled by rail from Chesterfield and other stations along the line to see local murderer, John Platts, hanged on top of the Derby county gaol.[221] Some railway companies even ran excursions to executions.[222] In Cornwall in 1840 the local railway company[223] ran special trains to the hanging of the Lightfoot brothers at Bodmin.[224] In September 1849 'the railway[s] turned the occasion [of the execution of the multiple murderer Gleeson Wilson at Liverpool] to a business

---

[219] V A C Gattrell, *The Hanging Tree*, OUP, 1994, p. 58; James Blomfield Rush murdered Isaac Jermy, the Recorder of Norwich, to whom he was heavily in debt, and the latter's brother. He shot his victims as they opened their front door and, disguised in a wig, mask and a long cloak, he escaped in the fog. Such was the notoriety of the case that his effigy was exhibited at Madame Tussauds for more than a century after his execution.

[220] Cf *The Times*, June 16, 1856 'The express trains and others from London on Friday night brought down a great number of well-dressed persons, but these bore no comparison…with the crowds which kept constantly arriving during the night by railway and other means of conveyance from the adjacent towns for 50 miles around including the Pottery districts, Birmingham, Wolverhampton, Walsall, Tipton and the rest of what is called the 'black country.' Three hundred and fifty constables were present to control the crowd, which was estimated by reporters at 50,000. Palmer was a doctor who sought to extricate himself from financial difficulty by poisoning his creditors and relatives, whose lives he had insured.

[221] *Sheffield Independent*, April 3, 1857; Platt, a Chesterfield butcher, murdered his business partner and then hid his body in nearby Bunting's Yard, where it lay undiscovered for nine months.

[222] Excursions had been run by railway companies from the earliest days. As early as 1831 the Midland Railway was carrying tens of thousands of passengers to race meetings on special trains In July 1841 Thomas Cook organised a rail excursion for 500 temperance campaigners from Leicester to Liverpool. Three years later a newspaper commented that excursions were becoming 'our chief national amusement.' Many of the six million visitors to the Great Exhibition of 1851 travelled there by excursion train.

[223] The Bodmin & Wadebridge Railway Company.

[224] Excursions or 'parties of pleasure' were run to an execution at Kirkdale prison, Liverpool in 1862 (PD 1864 vol 173 col 942 and 952).

purpose by running cheap trains every one of which was densely packed.'[225] To some this was taking public enthusiasm for excursions too far. Criticism in Parliament was particularly severe. In a debate on the death penalty in 1864, Lord Henry Lennox, having complained bitterly of

> *boards of railway directors, professing Christians no doubt, who advertised excursion trains or parties of pleasure from the manufacturing towns in order that the scum and refuse of their people might be conveyed to witness [public executions],*

said that the simplest way of putting a stop to the practice was to do what the authorities at Cambridge had done when the Whittlesea murderer was hanged, namely to bring forward the time of the execution without warning.[226] His advice was, however, largely ignored. Nor was abolishing excursions the answer. If there were no cheap fares available, people would travel by ordinary service train. When the Leeds murderer Dove was hanged at York in 1856 the regular trains were packed;[227] there was a good deal of complaint about the lack of cheap tickets but this had not deterred people from travelling and the railway company probably ended up making more money than it would have done from an excursion.

---

[225] *The Times*, September 17, 1849, quoting an article from *The Observer* (Wilson, after taking rooms in the house of a Mrs Henrichson, stole his landlady's jewellery and murdered her, her two sons aged five and two years and her servant Mary Pegg; he was tried and convicted at Liverpool Assizes on August 22, 1849 (*The Times*, August 24, 1849); according to *The Times* the lowest estimate of the size of the crowd was 100,000 of whom a considerable number were women, many respectably dressed).

[226] The High Sheriff had changed the time of execution from noon to 9 o'clock with the result that when the excursion trains arrived at Cambridge at half past 11 the culprit had already been dead for 2 ½ hours (PD (1856) vol 173 col 951).

[227] G Benson, *York from the Reformation to 1925*, Cooper & Swann, York, 1925, p 91.

The ending of public executions in 1868 deprived the public of the chance of seeing criminals hang (and stopped the railways profiting from the spectacle) but it did not lead to any decline in interest in executions, the populace remaining as fascinated as ever by the topic. Until reporters were excluded by the Home Office in the mid 1880s, most newspapers published detailed accounts of prison hangings and when this source of information dried up, others (such as autobiographies, and even public lectures, by hangmen) soon appeared.[228]

Nor did the tradition of people gathering outside prisons for executions die out. On a day when a criminal was due to hang, a crowd could usually be found at the prison gates waiting for the hoisting of the black flag and the posting of the notices of execution. Indeed, when the condemned was a notorious criminal or one whose plight had attracted public sympathy such crowds often began to gather as early as the execution eve.[229] In the twentieth century campaigners against the death penalty, such as the redoubtable Violet Van Der Elst,[230] were always present on

---

[228] In 1880, the year after Calcraft's death, *The Illustrated Police News* published in serial form *The Life and Recollections of Calcraft the Hangman*. In 1892 James Berry published his autobiography, *My Experiences as an Executioner* (Percy Lund, 1892), which he followed up with a lecture tour. After their retirement the memoirs of Harry Pierrepoint and John Ellis were serialised in *Thomson's Weekly News*. In 1927 Ellis appeared as hangman in a play at Gravesend Theatre. In 1974 A reprint of Ellis' memoirs was published in 1997 by Forum Press, London under the title *Diary of a Hangman*. In 1974 Albert Pierrepoint brought out his autobiography, *Executioner Pierrepoint* (Geo Harrop, London). 1989 saw the publication of S Dernley's *The Hangman's Tale* (Robert Hale, London); Dernley had worked for a short time as assistant to Pierrepoint.

[229] Cf G Ellis's description of the scene outside Holloway prison when her mother, Ruth Ellis, was executed in July 1955

'By first light the small crowd outside the prison gates which had kept an all night vigil had swelled to several hundreds and continued to grow with each ticking minute.'

Georgie Ellis, *Ruth Ellis, My Mother*, Smith Gryphon Ltd, London 1995, p. 212.

[230] Mrs Van Der Elst (referred to as VD by her detractors) was a millionairess who, for over 20 years, was an unflagging campaigner against the death penalty. She had attracted a great amount of

such occasions. When Derek Bentley was hanged at Wandsworth in 1953 an angry crowd of at least 1,000 stormed the prison gates and tore down the notices of execution; three men actually succeeded in getting inside the gaol and it was only with the greatest difficulty that police and prison officers were able to keep the rest back.

Nor was it only those outside the prison gates who kept checking the time as the fatal hour approached. When Derek Bentley and Ruth Ellis were hanged, in schools up and down the land all eyes were glued to the clock as it struck nine.

> *Today Ruth Ellis was hanged. Not only myself but many of my colleagues were faced with the effect of this upon the boys and girls we teach. The school was in a ferment... My colleagues and I agree that if there is any argument which weighs above all others for the abolition of capital punishment then it is this dreadful influence it had. For not only was Ruth Ellis hanged today, hundreds of children were corrupted. (The Times, July 14, 1955).*

Martha Browne's Body: A Wessex Tale

Martha Browne, a handsome woman who looked far younger than her 40 years, had met her husband, John, when they were fellow servants. After their marriage in 1851 he set up in business as a carrier, and it may be that it was her money which gave him his start. The gossips in Birdsmoorgate, Dorset where

---

press publicity since she made her debut outside the gates of Pentonville Prison on March 13, 1935 on the occasion of the hanging of Charles Lake for the murder of a bookmaker (on an execution day she would commonly sweep up to the prison in question in her Rolls Royce). She was the author of a book *On the Gallows*, Doge Press, 1937.

they lived said that he had married for money and given the difference in their ages – Martha was nearly 20 years his senior – it is not hard to understand why.

On July 5, 1856, Browne set out for Beaminster with his horse and cart in the company of another carter. After finishing work the two men repaired to a public house where they stayed drinking and playing skittles until late. It was around 2 a.m. when Browne arrived home[231] and, almost as soon as he got in, he and Martha set to rowing. She accused him of having been with a local girl named Mary Davis. For an answer he struck her across the face with his whip. For Martha, who had only recently caught him in bed with the Davis girl, this was the last straw. In a fury she picked up a hatchet and struck him several blows to the head. Three hours later, having disposed of the hatchet, she roused her neighbour, Damon. He hurried round to her cottage. On entering the living room he saw Browne lying on the floor dead, his head smashed in and his hair covered with brains and blood.[232]

'How did it happen?' he asked.

'I heard a noise outside, opened the door and found my husband bleeding heavily. He told me the horse had done it. I carried him along the passage into the living room.'

---

[231] About 2 in the morning a woman, named Knight, who lived close to the gate of the field in which the deceased kept his horse, heard the gate slam followed by the sound of a horse munching grass. Shortly afterwards, she heard footsteps going past her house. A Mrs Frampton, who lived some distance off, heard screams between 2 and 3 am coming from the direction of the Brownes' house.
[232] He had a broken nose, numerous wounds to the head and a fracture of the frontal bone, with no fewer than seven fragments of bone, varying from 3" to ½", driven into the brain.

'Why didn't you call me before?

'My husband had hold of my dress and I could not get away from him until he became weak and faint and I pushed him back and he fell to the ground.'

It was an improbable story. Had it been true there would have been a trail of blood leading from the field, where the horse was kept, to the door of the house and along into the living room, but there was none. The only place where there was blood was the room where the body lay.[233] The police, who did not swallow her explanation for a minute, charged Martha with murder.

She took her trial at Dorchester Assizes on July 21, 1856 before Mr Serjeant Channell.[234] She refused to change her story, leaving her counsel to argue somewhat desperately that her husband's death might have been caused by the kick of a horse, or that some third person might have inflicted his injuries but that it was unlikely his wife would have done so as she depended upon him for her living. After a retirement of just over four hours the jury returned with a verdict of guilty[235] and Martha was sentenced to death.

---

[233] The deceased's hat was found close to the field gate but it looked as if it had been placed there rather than fallen off. A halter was lying over the rails of the gate.
[234] *The Times*, July 23, 1856. Mr Block and Compton appeared for the prosecution. Mr Edwards defended.
[235] At 10 o'clock they had returned with a question. 'Could a man, with the head injuries which the deceased had, have, with assistance, got from the front door to the living room?' The surgeon was recalled. 'No, he could not,' was his answer. The verdict of guilty followed almost immediately.

While lying in the condemned cell awaiting execution, she finally confessed but her admission came too late to help her: there would be no reprieve. Had she told the truth from the beginning, it is possible that the trial judge might have recommended that her life be spared.

On the morning of August 9, 1856 she was brought out to die in front of Dorchester prison.[236] A crowd of between 3-4,000 had assembled in the rain to watch. At 8 o' clock, with the prison bell tolling, the main gate of the gaol opened and Martha, dressed in a black silk gown, emerged flanked by wardresses.

> *'On her way to the scaffold, her demeanour was extraordinary. The attendants on either side were overcome [but she] bore her awful position with great resignation and composure, [walking] with her hands clasped firmly together and her eyes upturned.'* [237]

To reach the scaffold itself she had to mount three flights of steps.[238] Still her courage did not fail. After pinioning her and adjusting the noose, Calcraft, the executioner, withdrew to operate the lever. Just as she was steeling herself for the drop, he returned to tie her skirt.[239] After the trap fell her body was left to hang for an hour before being cut down.

Present at the front of the crowd was Thomas Hardy, then a 16-year-old architect's clerk.[240] Accounts of the event which he

---

[236] In North Square. The site is now occupied by a car park. Unsuccessful attempts had been made to secure a reprieve. The execution (which was the last of a woman in the county) led the *Dorset Chronicle* to publish an article advocating the abolition of the death penalty.
[237] *The Times*, August 11 1856.
[238] The first flight had 11 steps, the second 19.
[239] To prevent it billowing up and exposing her legs.
[240] In 1858 Hardy witnessed at long distance through a telescope another Dorchester hanging, that of James Seale. This was the last public execution in Dorset. Afterwards Hardy crept home 'wishing he had not been so curious.'

gave in later life reveal that his reaction to it had 'a strong sexual component, focused not on the execution itself but on its immediate aftermath'[241]

> *'I remember what a fine figure she showed against the sky as she hung in the misty rain, and how the tight black silk gown set off her shape as she wheeled half-round and back.'* [242]
>
> *'The hanging itself did not move me. I sat on after the others went away, not thinking, but looking at the figure ... turning slowly round on the rope. And then it began to rain, and then I saw – they had put a cloth over the face – how as the cloth got wet her features came through it. That was extraordinary. A boy had climbed up into a tree nearby, and when she dropped, he came down in a faint like an apple dropping from a tree. It was curious the two dropping together.'* [243]

His erotic interest in the hanging of women was one which would surface in his writing. Thirty five years after Martha Browne's execution, Hardy 'would create in *Tess of the D'Urbervilles* one of the most vulnerable and attractive heroines in English fiction whose fate it is to be hanged'[244] and in 1923 on the eve of Edith Thompson's execution, as soon as he heard it confirmed that she was not to be reprieved, he celebrated the news with a poem entitled *'On the Portrait of a Woman about to be Hanged'*

---

[241] M Millgate, *Thomas Hardy: A Biography*, Random House, New York, 1982, pp. 62-63.
[242] Letter 20 January, 1926 from Hardy to Lady Pinney (quoted in her book, *Thomas Hardy and the Birdsmoorgate murder, 1856*, Beaminster, Dorset 1966).
[243] E Felkin, *Days with Thomas Hardy*, Encounter, April 1929
[244] Rene Weiss, *Criminal Justice*, Hamish Hamilton, London, 1988, p 291. Tess's execution, unlike that of Martha Browne, took place behind prison walls – see p 138 below. See also Robert Gittings, *The Young Thomas Hardy*, Heinemann, London, 1975, p 216 'The end of Tess on the scaffold where she pays the penalty of the law…echoes Hardy's adolescent experience of the death of Martha Brown[e].'

Comely and capable one of our race,
Posing there in your gown of grace,
Plain, yet becoming;
Could subtlest breast
Ever have guessed
What was behind that innocent face,
Drumming, drumming!

Would that your Causer, ere knoll your knell
For this riot of passion, might deign to tell
Why, since it made you
Sound in the germ,
It sent a worm
To madden its handiwork, when It might well
--Not have assayed you,

Not have implanted, to your deep rue,
The Clytaemnestra spirit in you,
And with purblind vision
Sowed a tare
In a field so fair,
And a thing of symmetry, seemly to view,
Brought to derision!

The Medical Hangman

Most of those employed as hangmen before 1886[245], if not actually criminals, were men of low character.[246] In 1884 *The*

---

[245] 'A low class of men prone to take stimulants' was the verdict of the Aberdare Committee of that year.

[246] In the eighteenth century two London hangmen were convicted of murder; one, Price, was executed, the other, named Thrift, pardoned and allowed to resume his duties. A third, Edward Dennis, was sentenced to death for his part in the Gordon Riots, 1780 (his career is described by Dickens in *Barnaby Rudge*). Another, Marvell, was arrested for debt as he was on his way to hang three felons at Tyburn, while a fifth, Cooper was dismissed for selling bodies to surgeons.

Barlow, who was the Lancaster hangman at the turn of eighteenth century, had twice been sentenced to transportation for life while, over at York, Currie who was the county's executioner from 1801 to 1835, had, like Barlow, taken the post to escape transportation and no fewer than three of his successors were like him prisoners or ex-prisoners.

Times opined that, while it did not follow that a man willing to execute criminals must be a blackguard, 'no man of refinement would undertake the [task].' But such a thing was not utterly unknown. In the 1860s and 1870s, as *The Times'* staff were well aware, Robert Ricketts Evans, the well-to-do son of a Carmarthenshire solicitor, had regularly acted as executioner and, in 1886, the activities of an Essex baronet would attract comment in both Parliament and press.

Evans, who later adopted the surname of Anderson,[247] was born in 1816. In his youth he had studied medicine for a time but had never qualified.[248] In the late 1850s he persuaded William Calcraft, who was then England's principal hangman, to take him on as an assistant. It was rumoured that he got the position by promising to give Calcraft his fees. Whatever the truth of this, there is no doubt that over the next 20 years he assisted Calcraft on many occasions and continued to do so right down to the latter's retirement in May 1874. The last execution which the pair ever conducted was that of James Edwin, hanged at Newgate on May 25, 1874 for the murder of his wife. In the National Library of Wales there is a letter to Anderson from the Governor of Newgate, dated May 11, 1874, which shows that it was Calcraft

---

Binns, who succeeded Calcraft as London hangman, was dismissed for drunkenness and, although the character of hangman improved after his dismissal in 1884, even in the twentieth century undesirables were still occasionally appointed (eg. the Nottinghamshire miner, Syd Dernley, author of *The Hangman's Tale*, who was dismissed for obscenity and was described by a journalist, who had the doubtful pleasure of meeting him, as giving the impression of 'truly revell[ing] in having killed ... with impunity' (Simon Jones, *Hanging out with Syd*, 1994).

[247] Possibly in an attempt to escape the nickname, Evans the Hangman, by which he was known in his native county.

[248] 'He had abandoned his studies in favour of a life of leisure and sensation-seeking,' James Bland, *The Common Hangman*. Zeon Books, Westbury, 2001, p 164. According to Bland, Evans married twice and boasted of many sexual conquests. He retained a keen interest in hanging until his death and was also an enthusiastic supporter of prize fights.

himself who had suggested that Anderson be employed on this occasion:

> *'The Sheriffs are very desirous that Calcraft shall have some assistance at an execution fixed for the 25th inst. and Calcraft named you as the person he wished to be with him and, unless you hear to the contrary, I shall expect to see you here on Saturday the 25th inst by 10 am.'*

But Evans was not merely an assistant. In the 1870s he conducted two triple executions as principal hangman, the first at Gloucester prison in January 1874,[249] the second at Liverpool the following year.[250] The latter was, it seems, the last hanging at which he officiated and, indeed, the last which he ever attended. His retirement was due, not to loss of appetite for the work, but to some falling out between himself and the prison authorities which led to *The Times* publishing in March 1875,[251] at his request, a letter which he had recently written to the Home Secretary. In it he gave an account of his career

> *For upwards of 20 years from humane motives I have devoted my attention to executions and have attended nearly all the principal executions that have taken place in this kingdom during that long period, giving my advice and assistance to the executioners, and in no single instance where I have been present has the slightest failure occurred or any unnecessary suffering been caused to the unfortunate culprit. In cases where I have occasionally acted alone – in triple executions for instance as at Liverpool and Gloucester – my plans have been completely successful. I submitted those plans to the prison*

---

[249] The execution on January 12, 1874 of 19-year-old Mary Ann Berry and her co-habitee for murder of their child and of Edward Butt for strangling his girl friend (*The Times*, January 13, 1874).

[250] The execution on January 4, 1875 of John M'crave and Michael Mullen for the murder of Richard Morgan, whom they had kicked to death, and of William Worthington for wife murder (*The Times*, January 5, 1875).

[251] December 11, 1875 11e.

authorities some years ago and, though they were disdainfully rejected, they have been subsequently adopted in one of the principal metropolitan and other prisons and found to be effective. My career has attracted the notice of the Press by which I have been styled 'the Amateur,' 'the Doctor,' the 'Medical Executioner' and other aliases [252] by writers who assumed to know my personal history. The fact is that I was intended for the medical profession but did not adopt it as I had private means. The taking part in this business has not been from mercenary but from humane motives, and it has cost me a large amount of time and money and has been a source of annoyance to some of my best friends

For Evans to claim that no unnecessary suffering had been caused at any of the executions at which he had acted as Calcraft's assistant takes some swallowing.[253] Calcraft was a notorious bungler who habitually gave his victims so short a drop that they strangled to death. Godwin, his last victim, took several minutes to die, during which his body was convulsed and he tried repeatedly to raise his hands to his throat.[254] His successor, Marwood, the proponent of the long drop left no one in any doubt of the contempt in which he held his predecessor: 'Calcraft hanged them. I execute them,' he boasted.

In 1884 Evans wrote to *The Times* again suggesting that the office of public hangman be abolished and that

---

[252] *The Times* generally referred to him as 'Calcraft's assistant,' see e.g. *The Times* January 13, 1874 11e and January 5, 1875 5f (the execution of M'crave and others) 'In this room they were pinioned by the executioner, who assumes the name of Anderson but is generally known as Calcraft's assistant.'

[253] It is perhaps revealing that Evans never condescended to explain what the technique of hanging which he had devised was, much less how it contributed to the efficiency and humanity of executions.

[254] Nor were the triple executions carried out by Anderson notable for their efficiency; of the trio he hanged at Gloucester, the woman certainly did not die instantaneously but ' lived some time longer than the others.' (*The Times*, January 13, 1874); at Liverpool he used a very short drop (2 ½ feet) and got away with it: 'the drop seemed quite sufficient to produce comparatively painless death as the bodies appeared scarcely to move after the trap doors fell.' (*The Times*, January 5, 1875).

executions should be performed by ... prison warders as part of their regular duty according to definite rules which [the Home Secretary] might draw up with proper medical and surgical advice. These rules should prescribe the way in which the condemned man should be pinioned, the length of the drop to be allowed and the position in which the knot or iron ring should be placed. With a simple rule on each of these points one warder would be perfectly competent to do what is necessary. To put a rope around a man's neck and to draw a lever are acts requiring no experience or manual dexterity. There is no more reason why a man should be brought from London to Liverpool to do such things than there is for bringing down a specially picked person to bury the prisoner's dead body.

Nor is there any reason to suppose that the warders would object. Many are already bound to be present if necessary. If one puts a rope over the prisoner's head and another pulled a lever they would not take a more direct part in the execution than they do at present.[255]

The suggestion was not taken up.[256]

In November 1886, hangman James Berry executed the Netherby Hall murderers, Rudge, Martin and Baker at Carlisle prison.[257] His assistant was a man calling himself Charles Maldon. When Berry and Maldon arrived at the prison on the night before the execution reporters were struck by how well dressed the assistant was. They were even more surprised when they later discovered that, rather than avail himself of the

---

[255] March 22, 1884 10e. The letter also dealt with the matter of why hangmen were generally held in contempt: 'I have speculations on the reason why an executioner is looked upon with disgust and aversion, whereas no one thinks the worse of a soldier forming one of a file who shoot a man condemned by a court martial. Surely the reason lies on the surface. The one man makes it his principal business to kill unresisting and helpless people at no risk to himself, the other does so only at long intervals and by accident, being as a rule otherwise employed. I think public sentiment would make exactly the same distinction between a warder, attending an execution as part of the routine duties of his position once in several years, and a man who has been successful in a disgusting and clamorous competition for the privilege of being the only man-butcher in the kingdom.'

[256] Evans died on August 26, 1901, aged 85 (for his obituary see the *Western Mail* (Cardiff) 28 August, 1901).

[257] The condemned men had shot four policemen, killing three, in the course of a burglary near the Scottish border.

accommodation provided at the prison, he had booked into the *County Hotel*, the best in town.[258] Suspecting that something strange was afoot, they made enquiries and quickly discovered that Maldon was in fact Sir Claude de Crespigny, a baronet, whose family seat was at Maldon in Essex.[259]

After the execution, Sir Claude was asked by reporters what he had been doing acting as assistant hangman? The explanation he offered was that, as a magistrate who was likely at some date in the future to become sheriff of his own county and responsible for executions there, he thought that he ought to experience the procedure himself before asking others to carry it out. He had approached Berry who was perfectly agreeable, especially after he had given him £10 for his trouble.[260] The press understandably had a field day with jokes in *Punch* about Lord McThrottle and the like. There was also a question in the House.[261] 'Was the Home Secretary aware that a baronet had assisted at a recent execution and, if so, what was his reaction to the disclosure?' It received a dusty answer: 'A baronet was as entitled as anybody to assist at an execution provided it were carried out properly.'[262]

---

[258] They also learned that there had been a rumpus at the hotel on the morning of the execution caused by Sir Claude's inviting Berry to take breakfast with him in the hotel dining room. Several guests complained to the management. They had no wish to take breakfast in the same room as a man who 'reeked of the gallows.' For the reporters this was manna from heaven.

[259] 'Sir Claude was a well known character in his day. A strong man, tales were told of his horse-whipping members of the Salvation Army, and boxing with his servants. He had even made an epic balloon flight, with a well known balloonist, Mr Simmons, from Lladon, across the Channel to Oudekerk near Flushing on 1 August, 1883; a distance of 140 miles covered in 6 hours. Indeed, it was said that he excelled in a variety of sports, and remained in later life 'one of the hardest and pluckiest men in England ... ready to box, ride, walk, run, shoot, fence, sail or swim and [one who] enjoyed a cold tub before breakfast.' Stewart P Evans, *Executioner*, Sutton Publishing, Stroud, 2004, p 93.

[260] Sir Claude disclosed to the press that he had previously attended another British execution, that of James Lee at Chelmsford gaol on May 18, 1885.

[261] From Sir Joseph Pease.

[262] Apparently Sir Claude performed his duties perfectly satisfactorily.

The last public hanging in Yorkshire [263]

April 6, 1868 dawned fine and bright in York. By 11 a.m. a sizeable crowd had already gathered in St George's Fields opposite the drop. As the Castle clock struck noon a hush fell over the spectators. Any second now the execution party would make its appearance on scaffold. York executions always drew a good crowd and for many of those assembled this hanging really was one not to be missed.[264] It was not the notoriety of the culprit which made it special (he was a 21-year-old, Frederick Parker, who had murdered a man for his money and his watch) but the fact that it would be the last ever public execution at York and in Yorkshire.[265] Going though Parliament at the time was the Capital Punishment Amendment Bill which, if passed, would abolish public executions.[266]

The clock had just stopped chiming when four halbardiers emerged from the door at the rear of the court house building. They were followed onto the scaffold by the under-sheriff, the prison governor, the chaplain, Parker, flanked by warders, the deputy governor, Askern, the hangman, and his assistant.

---

[263] See *The Times*, April 6, 1868, *Sheffield Independent*, April 6, 1868, *Sheffield Telegraph*, April 6, 1868 and *Hull and North Lincolnshire Times* April 8, 1868

[264] Estimates of the size of the crowd at the hanging varied from 5-6000 (not as many as usual) *Hull and North Lincolnshire Times*) to 8-10,000 (*Sheffield Independent*) to 10,000 (*Sheffield Telegraph*).

[265] The last ever public execution was that of the Fenian, Michael Barrett, at Newgate on May 26, 1868. Three other men were publicly executed in April and May, apart from Parker and Barrett. They were John Mapp (Shrewsbury, April 10), Richard Bishop (Maidstone, April 30), and Robert Smith (Dumfries, May 12).

[266] The Bill received the Royal Assent on May 29, 1868. S. 2 provided 'Judgment of death ... shall be carried into effect within the walls of the prison in which the offender is confined at the time of execution.'

Parker, having taken his place beneath the beam, shook hands with the governor, the under-sheriff and the warders and bade them good-bye. He hoped he would meet them in heaven where he was perfectly ready to go and he hoped Christ would accept him. He then knelt down and joined the chaplain in reciting the Lord's Prayer, after which the latter, having shaken his hand, left the platform. Askern, strikingly attired in a white waistcoat, now advanced. Parker's legs were pinioned, a white cap pulled over his head, the rope placed around his neck and the noose adjusted. The bolt was then drawn. The body fell with a loud thud, which could be heard in the crowd, and was lost to view.[267] Death was almost instantaneous, a slight convulsed twitching being all that was seen by those on the scaffold. An hour after the execution the body was cut down and buried within the precincts of the Castle prison.

According to the reporter from the *Sheffield Telegraph*, the execution of a man for murder never excited less sympathy in the watching crowd than did Parker's. If this be right, it is a little surprising. He was only 21; his crime was not especially heinous; he appeared genuinely remorseful and, in his short life, had had his share of misfortune.

He was born at Leeds in March 1847. Within a week of his birth both his parents were dead. He was taken in and brought up by his uncle, Thomas Parker, a small farmer at Hemingbrough in the East Riding. Unhappily he was to prove a disappointment to

---

[267] *Hull and North Lincolnshire Herald*, April 8, 1868 'The railing around the scaffold was for the first time draped with a black cloth and the consequence was that, as soon as the trap fell, the culprit was screened from the view of the multitude in front of the drop.'

his uncle. At age of ten, at the East Riding Quarter Sessions, he was committed to the Beverley House of Correction for a month for attempting to derail a train on the Market Weighton to Selby line, by placing wood on the rails. In his teens he was committed to the Wakefield House of Correction for stealing cloth. On his release he joined the Pontefract militia. By now he had developed a taste for drink and was drinking heavily. In December 1867 he was convicted of stealing fowls and sentenced to two months in the Beverley House of Correction. He was released from prison on February 29, 1868 along with 27- year-old, Daniel Driscoll.

On leaving the jail, Driscoll went to the *Red Lion* public house, where he was joined within minutes by Parker. Driscoll, who was wearing a silver watch chain, told the landlord in Parker's presence that he had four sovereigns on him. After spending two hours drinking, the pair set off for Bubwith, 18 miles away, which they reached at around 7 p.m. There they called in at a public house for ale for which Driscoll paid. They left saying they were going to Hemingbrough. This was the last time Driscoll was seen alive. At 9 the next morning his body was found some three miles away in a ditch at the side of the road. Lying close by it was a bloodied hedge stake. His silver watch was missing as was his gold.

That same day Parker tried to sell the watch and, finding no takers, hid it in a hedge bottom from where it was later recovered by the police. He also made a gift of four sovereigns and 4s and 6d in silver to a friend, a surprising act of generosity on the part of a man who had only had 1s 4½d on him when released from prison the previous day. He was arrested on March 5 and fifteen days later stood trial for Driscoll's murder at York Assizes.[268] He was convicted and sentenced to death.

After his trial Parker seemed indifferent both to his crime and his fate but, as the day of his execution approached, his attitude changed. For the first time he began to express remorse for what he had done and paid great attention to the ministrations of the prison chaplain.

On the day of execution, he rose at quarter to six and having dressed spent the next quarter of an hour in prayer. At 8 o' clock he took holy communion in the prison chapel. At 10 o'clock he attended the morning service during which, at his particular request, the hymn *'Brief life is here our portion'* was sung. At 11 30 he was removed from the condemned cell to a room near the drop. Before leaving the cell he went down on his knees and cried aloud 'Lord Jesus, have mercy on my soul so that in a few minutes I hope to be with Thee and how joyful and happy it is to have it so near to be with my Lord.' At 5 to 12 he was pinioned and, on the under sheriff's arriving and demanding his body for execution, he was conducted to the scaffold. He appeared calm and resigned and walked onto the drop with a firm step. Just before the time for execution he handed to the Governor a letter which he had written to his friends at Hemingbrough, calling on

---

[268] The trial judge was Mr Justice Smith. Messrs Thomson and Peel appeared for the prosecution. Samuel Danks Waddy, (later Recorder and County Court judge of Sheffield) defended. For an account of the trial, which was held on March 20, see *The Times*, March 21, 1868.

them to benefit from his fate and warning against drink which he said had brought him to his present position.[269]

An odd feature of the case is that a couple of days after the murder he was due to receive a legacy of £21 left to him by his father.

York Private Executions

The first hanging carried out at York, following the abolition of public executions in May, 1868, was that of William Jackson on August 18, 1874. Most prisons at this time were still using portable scaffolds[270] but not so York. There, following the enactment of the Capital Punishment Amendment Act, a drop had been built in a cell in the old Women's Prison. The reports in the York newspapers of Jackson's execution gave a full description of the new gallows

> *After the passing of the [Act of 1868] the old scaffold used at executions was of no further use [and] was abandoned and taken to pieces. The old wood was, however, made available for the construction of a new drop, which is of a much smaller size than its predecessor and is placed in a large cell fitted up for its reception adjoining the condemned cell. The end wall of the drop cell has been taken out and folding doors substituted, whilst the new drop is firmly fixed by bolts on the flooring and it can be easily turned forward, by means of massive hinges, when the folding doors are open, until it projects forward into*

---

[269] The letter was addressed to the Bandmaster of Hemingbrough) and asked that it be read out to his friends (Parker had at one time been a member of the band).

[270] See e.g. the following *Times* reports of executions: March 31, 1869 (Strangeways); August 13, 1869 (Portland); October 12, 1869 (Exeter); December 14, 1869 (Newgate); April 2, 1872 (Lincoln); and August 13, 1872 (Worcester). A portable scaffold erected in the prison yard was used for executions at Armley from 1868 to 1887 (see D. Bentley, *The Sheffield Murders*, ALD Shefield, 2003, p. 15).

> *the open air, when the platform on which the culprit has to stand is about eight feet from the ground below. The front of the stage or platform is protected by a light iron railing and the fatal beam above is kept firmly in place by two strong chains, one fixed at each end, which are very tight when the drop is put in working order. These chains are held by iron rings and staples inserted in lead on the stone floor. The drop is made to fall by a strong lever similar to those used at points on railways and the culprit, whilst hanging, is from three to four feet above the ground below. When the drop has been done with for the time, it can be turned round into its former position, the operation being something like shutting the lid of a box. The folding doors are next shut and the cell closed, the apparatus of death being ready again when the unhappy time arrives for another execution.*[271]

Between 1874 and 1900 a total of ten murderers were executed at York Castle prison. Of these the majority came from the East and North Ridings. Two, however, were from South Yorkshire.[272]

Until 1880 newspaper reporters were normally admitted to executions at the prison but the practice was stopped in 1886.[273]

Tuesday was the usual execution day.[274] A quarter of an hour before an execution (most took place at 8 am) the bell of St Mary, Castlegate began to toll and would continue to do so for half an hour. As soon as the drop fell a signal would be given to a prison officer on Clifford's Tower, who would immediately run a

---

[271] *York Gazette*, August 22, 1874; the *York Herald*, August 19, 1874; contained a similar account. See also I P Pressley, *The Castle of York*, York Corpn 1950, p 23 'When public executions ceased outside the prison it was here [the female prison] they were carried out ...the present Curator's office was the cell from which the condemned stepped on to the fatal drop.'

[272] They were John Henry Wood, executed on May 14, 1880 for the murder of John Coe at Catcliffe near Rotherham, and James Murphy, executed on December 4, 1886 for the murder of a police officer at Dodworth near Barnsley; after 1864 West Riding murderers were normally tried and executed at Leeds; unusually Wood and Murphy were both tried and hanged at York.

[273] They were not admitted to the execution of John Darcy in May 1879 but were present when John Henry Wood was hanged the following May.

[274] Of the ten executions carried out between 1874 and 1896, eight took place on a Tuesday and two on a Monday.

black flag up the flag pole.[275] After hanging for an hour the convict's body would be cut down and placed in an open coffin to await inspection by the inquest jury.[276] Following the inquest it would be buried in the prison yard in an area close by the drop.[277] (Before 1868 the practice had been to inter the bodies of executed murderers in a patch of ground at the back of the old County Gaol).

The last person to be hanged at the prison was August Carlsen executed in December, 1896. Less than four years later the prison was closed.[278] Following the closure, Hedon Road prison, Hull was made the hanging prison for the East Riding[279] and Armley prison used for North Riding executions.

---

[275] The flag would be flown until the body was cut down.

[276] After Murphy's execution, the inquest jury were taken 'to view the scaffold and the body. They were conducted along passages until a sudden turn to the left through the door of a cell brought the scaffold into full view. The outer wall of the cell which abuts upon the murderers' burial ground had been knocked out and replaced by folding doors which open outwards.' (*York Gazette*, December 4, 1886).

[277] Cf the *York Gazette* report of Walker's execution: 'the remains of the murderer were interred in the graveyard for murderers, a small piece of ground set aside for the purpose near to the condemned cell within the precincts of the castle.' See also the *Gazette* report of Murphy's execution (above) 'Murphy's dead body in the clothes which he wore at his trial had been placed in an ordinary wooden coffin in the bottom of which had been placed quicklime and [which] was laid on the ground just below the scaffold whilst a few yards away was the grave in which his remains would be buried.' According to executioner Berry, Murphy on spying the open grave turned to him and said 'Yon's where I'm going to sleep tonight' (Stewart P Evans, *Executioner*, p 122).

[278] See T.P. Cooper, *York Castle*, 1911, p 244 'York Castle by the decision of the Home Secretary and his advisers ceased to be a civil prison on July 31, 1900. The prisoners were removed to Wakefield Gaol and the Governor of York, Mr Edwin Taylor, transferred to Northallerton. The vacated prison was immediately taken over by the military authorities, under licence from the Prison Commissioners and under the sanction of the Home Department, to be utilized as a Military Detention barracks.'

[279] The use of the Hedon Road jail was not without its difficulties. Hull murderers continued to be tried at York and, since it was the practice to take them there by train, a murderer who had just been convicted and sentenced to death could and often did find himself travelling back to Hull in the same train as his victim's relatives, the press and witnesses who had given evidence against him at trial (See A. Young, *More Hull Murders*, Highgate Press, Beverley, 1996, p 26 'A normal passenger service was used and on several occasions the same train would often carry the prisoner, the prison guards, his family, relatives of the victim, witnesses who gave evidence at the trial and the inevitable newspaper reporters. On arrival at Paragon railway station, large crowds would gather to catch a glimpse of the prisoner as he was transferred to a waiting cab, cheering or jeering depending on whether the death sentence was considered justified.')

Executions in literature

The place in England which saw more hangings than any other was London's Tyburn. There had been a gallows there since at least the thirteenth century and until 1783 it was used with relentless regularity for public executions.[280] Dr Johnson made reference to the numbers despatched in his poem *London*

> **Scarce can our Fields, such Crowds at Tyburn die,**
> **With Hemp the Gallows and the Fleet supply**

On an execution day[281] (until 1834 there were eight a year) the under-sheriffs of London and Middlesex would attend at Newgate prison and demand the bodies of those who were to die; the condemned would be brought from their cells, have their shackles struck off and then be taken to a waiting cart containing their coffins. The cart would set off turning west as it left Newgate Street past the Church of St Sepulchre.[282] Up towards Holborn it would climb, along Holborn and Oxford Street to what is now Marble Arch but was then open fields. There waiting stood the triple tree, a gallows consisting of three upright posts set in triangle with connecting cross beams above. A vivid picture of the

---

[280] One of the earliest literary descriptions of a London hanging (albeit not at Tyburn) is to be found in Samuel Pepys' *Diary* 'At noon, going to the Change and seeing people flock in that direction, I enquired and found that Turner was not yet hanged and so I went among them to Leadenhall Street at the end of Lyme Street, near where the robbery was done and to St Mary Axe where he lived; and there I got for a shilling to stand upon the wheel of a cart, in great pain, above an hour before the execution was over, he delaying the time by long discourses and prayers one after another in the hope of a reprieve, but none came and at last [he] was flung off the ladder' (Entry for January 21, 1663).
[281] After 1834 there twelve.
[282] There would be prostitutes outside the church with nosegays for the condemned.

journey to Tyburn is given by Swift in his poem ***Clever Tom Clinch going to be hanged (1727)***

> **As clever Tom Clinch while the mob was howling**
> **Rode stately through Holborn to die of his Calling**
> **He stopt at the George for a Bottle of Sack**[283]
> **And promised to pay for it when he came back**
>
> **His waistcoat and stockings and breeches were white**
> **His cap had a new cherry ribbon to tie't**
> **The maids to their doors and the balconies ran**
> **And said Lack a day he's a proper young man**
> **But as from the windows the ladies he spied**
> **Like a beau he bowed low on each side**
>
> **The hangman for pardon fell down on his Knee**
> **Tom gave him a kick in the guts for his fee**
>
> **Follow the practice of clever Tom Clinch**
> **who hung like a hero and never would flinch**

Clinch was almost certainly a highwayman and it was a matter of honour with such men to die game.

When Jack Sheppard, who had twice escaped from Newgate and was the darling of the London mob, was hanged in 1724 he died bravely plotting escape to the end. When Turpin was executed at the York Tyburn on a summer's day in 1739, like Tom Clinch, he took considerable pains, decking himself out with a new coat and pumps; he paid five poor men 10s each to follow

---

[283] It was the custom for the cart to stop at *The George* in Holborn and *The Bowl* on the corner of St Giles High Street for the condemned to take wine and ale.
(cf York - there, in 1649, as the Merringtons were being taken to St Leonard's gallows for execution, the cart stopped and wine was sent for from a nearby ale house; legend has it that the life of a Bawtry saddler would have been saved if he had taken the ale offered to him along the route (it is said that a reprieve was on its way and, had he stopped to take the customary bowl of ale, it would have arrived in time to save his life).

the cart as mourners and, as it slowly made its way from the Castle over the Ouse up Micklegate and out towards the Knavesmire, he stood erect in the cart bowing gravely to the crowd. His final moments are described in the **York Courant**

> *it was very remarkable that, as he mounted the ladder, his right leg trembled on which he stampt it down and, with undoubted courage, looked around him and, after speaking a few words to the Topsman, he threw himself off the ladder and expired in about five minutes*[284]

A number of contemporary paintings and drawings of London's Tyburn survive of which that from Hogarth's *Idle Apprentice* is perhaps the best known. But we also have literary descriptions including these entries for May 1763, in Boswell's *London Journal*.[285]

Tuesday, 3 May

> *I walked up to the Tower in order to see Mr Wilkes come out. But he was gone. I then thought I should see prisoners of one kind or another and so went to Newgate. I stepped into a sort of court before the cells. They are surely the most dismal places. There are three rows of them, four in a row, all above each other. In the cells were Paul Lewis for robbery and Hannah Diego for theft. I saw them pass by to chapel. The woman was a big unconcerned being. Paul, who had been in the sea service, and was called Captain, was a genteel, spirited young fellow. He was just a MacHeath. He*

---

[284] Turpin's career like that of Sheppard would later become the subject of a novel by Harrison Ainsworth
[285] Reprint Society, London, 1950, 245-246.

was dressed in a white coat and blue silk vest and silver, with his hair neatly queued and a silver-laced hat, smartly cocked. He walked firmly and with a good air with his chains rattling upon him to the chapel.

Wednesday, 4 May

My curiosity to see the melancholy spectacle of the execution was so strong that I could not resist it. I wished to see the last behaviour of Paul Lewis, the handsome fellow I had seen the day before. I took Captain Temple with me and he and I got upon a scaffold very near the fatal tree so that we could see clearly all the dismal scene. There was a most prodigious crowd of spectators. I was most terribly shocked and thrown into a deep melancholy.

The other eighteenth century work in which Tyburn features heavily is John Gay's *Beggar's Opera*. McHeath, the play's hero, is a highwayman determined to die bravely as the following two airs (one sung as he is about to be taken to the Old Bailey for his trial and the other after sentence)[286] demonstrate

The charge is prepared the lawyers are met
The judges all ranged (a terrible show)
I go undismayed, For death is a debt
A debt on demand. So take what I owe

Since I must swing, I scorn, I scorn to whince or whine

As the play nears its end, one of the players says to the author 'I hope you don't intend MacHeath shall be really executed.' After insisting that he does he eventually relents and

---

[286] John Gay, *The Beggar's Opera*, Penguin Books, London, 1986, pp. 115-16, and 117

cries out '**You rabble there – run and cry a reprieve.**'[287] The ending was not, however, to everyone's taste. According to Serjeant Robinson the only time Baron Gurney, a hard faced nineteenth-century judge, had been known to shed a tear was when it was announced on stage that McHeath was reprieved.[288]

---

[287] Ibid. pp 120-121. Last minute reprieves were not uncommon. In 1705 a burglar, named Smith, had already been hanging for 15 minutes when a reprieve arrived and he was cut down and revived The reason for his survival was the then universal practice of giving culprits a 'short drop' (no more than a few feet); this was not sufficient to fracture the neck and condemned man usually strangled to death. Cf the following description of execution of John Tawell at Aylesbury, March 28, 1845

> **The length of drop allowed him was so little that he struggled violently. His whole frame was convulsed; he writhed horribly and his limbs rose and fell again repeatedly while he wrung his hands, his arms having previously been pinioned, and he continued to wring his hands for several minutes, they still being clasped as though he had not left off praying. It was nearly ten minutes after the rope had been fixed before the contortions which indicated extreme suffering ceased.**

The reason why Turpin threw himself off the ladder was probably to avoid being slowly strangled; it was a common trick. At Strabane, in 1761, John M'Naughten tried a violent jump but the rope broke and he had to wait until a man who had been hanged with him was dead so that the rope, used to hang the latter, could be re-used.

After his narrow escape Half-hanged Smith gave the following account of his ordeal, which is one of the few descriptions of what it felt like to be hanged:

> when he was turned off, he, for some time, was sensible of very great pain occasioned by the weight of his body and felt his spirits in a great commotion violently pressing upwards; that having forced their way to his head he, as it were, saw a great blaze or glaring light, which seemed to go out at his eyes with a flash and he lost all sense of pain. That after he was cut down and began to come to himself, the blood and spirits forcing themselves into their former channels, put him to such intolerable pain that he wished he could have hanged those who cut him down

[288] Serjeant Robinson, *Bench and Bar*, Hurst & Blackett, London, 1889, p 158.

The End of Tyburn

In 1783, in order to limit the public disorder and obstruction to traffic caused by executions, the city authorities decided to discontinue the use of Tyburn. Henceforth executions would take place outside Newgate, using a portable scaffold put up specially on each occasion. One person who protested at the change was Dr Johnson. 'It is not, Sir, an improvement,' he told Boswell.

> *They object that the old method drew together a number of spectators. Sir, executions are intended to draw spectators. If they don't draw spectators they don't answer their purpose. The old method was most satisfactory to all parties. The public was gratified by the procession. The criminal was supported by it.*[289]

Descriptions of Newgate hangings abound. One of best known is **Thackeray's** essay **'Going to see a man hanged'** The hanging described is that of Francois Courvoisier, executed Monday July 6, 1840, for cutting the throat of his elderly employer, Lord William Russell:

> *Courvoisier walked very firmly. His arms were tied in front of him. He opened his hands in a helpless kind of way and clasped them once or twice together. He turned his head here and there and looked about him for an instant with a wild imploring look....He went and placed himself at once under the beam with his face towards St Sepulchre's. The tall grave man in black twisted him round swiftly in the other direction and, drawing from his pocket a night cap, pulled it tight over the patient's head and face.*

---

[289] James Boswell, *Life of Johnson*, vol IV, pp. 188f.

I am not ashamed to say that I could look no more but shut my eyes as the last dreadful act was going on which sent this wretched guilty soul into the presence of God

Coventry Patmore's poem *A London Fete* **1853,** provides another:

The scaffold built at 8 o' clock
They brought the man out to be hanged
Then came from all the people there
A single cry that shook the air
Mothers held up their babes to see
Who spread their hands and crowed for glee

At last the show's crisis pended
Thousands of eyeballs lit with hell
burnt one way all, to see the rope unslacken
as the platform fell
The rope flew tight and then the roar
burst forth afresh, less loud

Dickens, who, like Thackeray, was a spectator at Courvoisier's execution had a lively interest in public hangings. He was fully familiar with the condemned cells at Newgate, which he had seen during a private tour of the prison and, in *Oliver Twist*, he drew on this knowledge when describing Fagin's last night on earth

they led him to one of the condemned cells, and left him there – alone. He sat down on a stone bench opposite the door, which served for seat and bedstead[290]

---

[290] *Oliver Twist*, chapter 52.

Among his most powerful contributions to the literature are two passages in *Barnaby Rudge* (one of his least successful novels), in which he describes the execution of some of those who had taken part in the Gordon riots in 1780:

> *Two cripples both mere boys – one with a leg of wood, one who dragged his twisted limbs along by the help of a crutch, were hanged in this same Bloomsbury square. As the cart was about to glide from under them, it was observed that they stood with their faces from, not to, the house they had assisted to despoil and their misery was protracted that this omission might be remedied.*[291]

> *One young man was hanged in Bishopsgate Street whose aged, grey-headed father waited for him at the gallows, kissed him at its foot when he arrived, and sat there, on the ground, until they took him down. They would have given him the body of the child, but he had no hearse, no coffin, nothing to remove it in, being too poor and walked meekly away beside the cart that took it back to prison, trying as he went to touch its lifeless hand*[292]

Private Executions

1868 saw the end of public executions, it being provided by the Capital Punishment Amendment Act of that year that henceforth all executions must take place inside prisons. The sheriff was given power to admit spectators and the Act also incorporated a number of provisions designed to ensure that full

---

[291] *Barnaby Rudge*, Penguin Books Ltd., London, 2003 p 649. The house in question was the town house of Lord Chief Justice Mansfield.
[292] Ibid. p. 648. The passage finds an echo in *The Reminiscences of Sir Henry Hawkins* (ed Harris), Nelson & Sons, London, 1904, p. 15 'I saw emerging from a by-street that led from Bedford Jail ...a common farm cart, drawn by a horse which was led by a labouring man...behind walked a poor, sad couple with their heads bowed down, and each with a hand on the tail board of the cart. They were evidently overwhelmed with grief. ...The cart contained the rude shell into which had been laid the body of the poor man and woman's only son, a youth of seventeen, hanged that morning at Bedford Jail for setting fire to a stack of corn.'

publicity was given to the fact of execution: before a hanging the prison bell was to be rung and, immediately after it had taken place, a black flag was to be run up; an inquest was to be held on the body of the culprit and notices posted at the prison gate certifying the fact that an execution had taken place and that an inquest had been held.[293] Until the mid-1880s it was the practice of most sheriffs to admit the press and we have, accordingly, numerous press accounts of prison hangings. The best known literary descriptions of the new order are those to be found in Hardy's *Tess of the D'Urbervilles* and Oscar Wilde's *Ballad of Reading Gaol*.

Hardy

When Angel and Lisa Lu reached the top of the great West Hill the clocks in the town struck eight. Each gave a start at the notes. The prospect from this summit was almost unlimited. In the valley beneath lay the city they had just left. In front of the other city edifices rose a large red bricked building with level grey roofs and rows of short barred windows bespeaking captivity…From the middle of the building an ugly flat-topped octagonal tower ascended…Upon the cornice of this tower a tall staff ascended. Their eyes were riveted upon it. A few minutes after the hour had struck something moved slowly up the staff and extended itself upon the breeze. It was a black flag.
Justice was done and the President of the Immortals had ended his sport with Tess.[294]

---

[293] These provisions were designed to meet an objection which had constantly been raised to private executions, namely that the public would never believe that rich and influential offenders had in fact been executed (*The Times*, July 17, 1856 '[It] would be construed as class legislation against the common people; the working class would refuse to believe that influential well to do offenders would not escape punishment.')
[294] *Tess of the D'urbervilles*, Penguin Books, London 1994, pp 507-08.

Wilde

At six o' clock we cleaned our cells
At seven all was still.
but the sough and swing of a mighty wind
The prison seemed to fill
For the Lord of Death with icy breath
Had entered in to kill

So they kept us close till nigh on noon
And then they rang the bell
And the Warders with their jingling keys
Opened each listening cell

The warders strutted up and down
Their uniforms were spick and span
They wore their Sunday best
But we knew the work they had been
at by the quick lime on their boots

for where a grave had opened wide
There was no grave at all
Only a stretch of mud and sand
By the hideous prison wall
And a little heap of burning lime
That man should have his pall[295]

---

[295] Wilde in a letter to Robert Ross had written that 'the shed in which people are hanged is a little shed with a glass roof like a photographer's studio on the sands at Margate.' He was an accurate observer: compare the above passage with this taken from the **Sheffield Independent** for August 23, 1887:

the culprit was buried in one of the exercising yards as the back of the gaol where eight other unfortunate men who have been executed there have previously been interred. All preparations for the speedy interment of the body had been made and, within an hour after the jury had found their verdict, the corpse was deposited in the unnamed grave. The surface of the exercising yard is perfectly level and there are no indications, save private marks known to the gaol officials, where any of the bodies lay

One of the last nineteenth-century literary references to capital punishment is this passage in Arnold Bennett's *The Old Wives Tale*

On the Sunday morning after the day on which The Signal had printed the menu of Daniel Povey's supreme breakfast and the exact length of the drop which the executioner had administered to him, Constance and Cyril stood together at the window of the large bedroom. 'Oh mother,' Cyril exclaimed suddenly. 'Listen I'm sure I can hear the band.' The music appeared to linger a long time in the distance and then it approached, growing louder, and the Bursley Town Silver Prize Band passed under the window at the solemn pace of Handel's Dead March.

The bandsmen were not all in black but they all wore crepe on their sleeves and their instruments were knotted with crepe. They carried in their hats a black edged card Cyril held one of these cards in his hand. It ran thus

> *Sacred to the memory of Daniel Povey*
> *A Town Councillor of this Town*
> *Judicially Murdered at 8 o' clock in the morning*
> *8th February, 1888*
> *He was more sinned against than sinning.*

In the wake of the band came the aged Rector bareheaded and wearing a surplice over his overcoat. A curate, churchwardens and sidesmen followed. After these, tramping through the dark mud in a procession that had apparently no end, wound the unofficial male multitude nearly all in mourning.[296]

---

[296] *The Old Wives Tales*, Penguins Books, London, 1963, p 269.

The twentieth century saw a number of hangmen publish autobiographies,[297] several anti-hanging polemics, such as Violet Van Der Elst's *On the Gallows* and true crime biographies, without number, but little else.[298]

---

[297] The reminiscences of Harry Pierrepoints and John Ellis were published in serial form in *Thomson's Weekly News*; see also A Pierrepoint, *Executioner Pierrepoint*, Harrop, London 1974, and Syd Dernley, *The Hangman's Tale*, Robert Hale, London, 1989.
[298] The Doge Press, London, 1937.

INDEX

Allen, James 15, 22
Anatomy Act 24, 25
Armitage, Harold 24
Armley prison 45

Bakewell 38
Ballad of Reading Gaol 163
Ballantine, Serjeant 84,118
Banks, Nellie 98, 99
Barnaby Rudge 162
Barrington, Sir Jonah 65-73
Bradfield Watch House 24
Bedford Assizes 109
Beggar's Opera 158
Bennett, Arnold 165
Boswell, James 157, 158
Brandreth, Jeremiah 3-12
Browne, Martha 137-141
Burke and Hare 24
Butterley 5-6

Calcraft 143-145
Chartism 12-13
County court 87
County court judges
  Walker 88
Coroner, office of 73,82
  Nottingham 96-98
  Shropshire 73-82
Cork Assizes 105-106
Court funds, scandals
  concerning 71-73

De Crespigny, Sir C 146
Denman, Lord 37-42
Derby
  Church of St Werburgh 10
  Nuns' Green 10
Dernley, Syd 143, 166
Dickens, Charles 83, 161-162
Dove 135

Ecclesall Gaol 35-36
Ellis, John 54
Ellis, Ruth 137
Evans, Robert Ricketts 143-146

Frost, John 13,19

Gallagher 46-54
Gay, John 158
Giltbrook 7

Hardy, Thomas 140-142, 163
Harrold 107
Hatch, Rev Henry 113-129
Holberry, Samuel 12-22
Hogarth 157
Howard, John 33
Hull
  Assizes 55
  Gallows 55, 154
  Prison 55, 154

Irish marriages 105-107

James, Edwin QC 122-124
Johnson, Dr Samuel 155, 160

Judges
  Abbott, J 8
  Best, J 78
  Channell, B 125
  Charles, J 59
  Dallas, J 8
  Darling, J 52
  Erskine, J 19
  Gaselee, J 83
  Graham, B 109
  Holroyd, J 8
  Hullock, B 79
  Johnson, J (Irish) 81-82
  Lopes, J 96
  Mellor, J 29
  Pennefather, B (Irish) 106
  Richards, CB 8
  Watkin Williams J 96-99

Laing, Alan 83-87
Lancaster Castle prison 93
Leeds Mercury 11
Lewis & Lewis 118, 126-127
Lightfoot brothers 134
Limerick Assizes 105
Liverpool Journal 90-91
Livesey, Rev 29-32

Major, Ethel 55-61
Marriages in judge's
  room 105-106
Marwood, Wm 145
Monmouth rising 13

Newton, John 73-78
Northallerton House of
  Correction 20
Nottingham
  Judges' Lodgings 155
  North Street 97-98

Oliver, the spy 4, 10-11
Old Wives Tale, The 165
Oliver Twist 84, 161
Overend, Hall 23-27

Paine, Dr 85-87
Palmer, Dr Wm 134
Paradise Square 13-14
Parker, Frederick 148-152
Pentridge (Pentrich) 4-6
Pickwick Papers 83
Pierrepoint, Thomas 61
Platts, John 134
Plummer, Eugenia 13-126
Prince Regent 3, 10

Queen Caroline's Case 39-40

Ramshay, Wm 87-95
Rape compromises 103-107
Raynor, Thomas 15-16
Ripley 6
Railway excursions 134-135
Rush, James 134

Sheffield riots
  1791 34
  1835 25-27
  1862 27-28
Sheffield Medical School 23-27
Sheffield gaol 33-36
Sheffield general
  Cemetery 21-22

Sheffield streets

Arundel Street 23
Bennet Street 16
Bishop Street 33
Carver Street 16
Church Street 23, 26
Crookesmoor 16
Eyre Lane 16
Eyre Street 25
Figtree Lane 14
Glossop Road 17
Infirmary Road 17
King Street 33-35
Livesey Street 31
Scotland Street 34-35
Surrey Street 23
Tudor Street 33
Watery Lane 16

Shrewsbury Assizes 78-79
South Wingfield 5
Stoney Middleton Hall 37
Swann, Emily 45-55, 40-42
Swanwick 5
Swift, Jonathan 156

*Tess of the
 D'Urbervilles 141, 163*
Thackeray, Wm M 160
Thurtell, John 133
Tyburn 155-162

Van der Elst, Violet 61, 166

Westbury, Lord Chancellor 72-73
Whitecombe, Edward 73-81

White Horse, Pentridge 4-5
Whitty, Michael J 91-94
Wightman, Dossey 49
Wilde, Oscar 163-164
Woodward, Rev Robert 107-113

York castle prison
  Castle drop 148
  Clifford's Tower 153
  Private executions at 152-4
  St George's Fields 148
  St Mary's Castlegate 153
York Courant 157